TAROT
IS A
HEALING ART

DEVELOP YOUR WISDOM AND
UNLEASH YOUR POWER

ZACHARY D. WEAVER, PhD
DR. Z

BALBOA.PRESS

A DIVISION OF HAY HOUSE

Balboa Press books may be ordered through booksellers or by contacting:

Balboa Press
A Division of Hay House
1663 Liberty Drive
Bloomington, IN 47403
www.balboapress.com
844-682-1282

Because of the dynamic nature of the Internet, any web addresses or links contained in this book may have changed since publication and may no longer be valid. The views expressed in this work are solely those of the author and do not necessarily reflect the views of the publisher, and the publisher hereby disclaims any responsibility for them.

The author of this book does not dispense medical advice or prescribe the use of any technique as a form of treatment for physical, emotional, or medical problems without the advice of a physician, either directly or indirectly. The intent of the author is only to offer information of a general nature to help you in your quest for emotional and spiritual well-being. In the event you use any of the information in this book for yourself, which is your constitutional right, the author and the publisher assume no responsibility for your actions.

Any people depicted in stock imagery provided by Getty Images are models, and such images are being used for illustrative purposes only. Certain stock imagery © Getty Images.

Interior Image Credit: Joseph Hawkins

Print information available on the last page.

ISBN: 978-1-9822-5142-0 (sc)
ISBN: 978-1-9822-5143-7 (hc)
ISBN: 978-1-9822-5141-3 (e)

Library of Congress Control Number: 2020913039

Balboa Press rev. date: 08/22/2020

For my "First Mother," my grandmother Mary Lanier Weaver (a.k.a. GG), the Queen of Wands. I am, as a result of your sacrifice. I love you. May your memory live on through me.

Table of Figures

Contents

Chapter 1

Lost in the Sauce

Are you lost in the sauce? You're existing in a world busy with the hustle and bustle and the pursuit of material gain, the evidence of would-be worldly success. The pressure of it all can be overwhelming. The endless campaign of accomplishment and bills presses down upon you, demanding satisfaction. You are ever reminded to fulfill those external expectations. The external pressures have now been internalized and become part of the identified self.

The world is in your hands, but it hardly feels that way. There's a constant movement of people, expectations, and required responsibility thrust upon you. The world, as you know it, hardly seems yours at all. The world seems to have a preset program already installed, a default framework. We are programmed to believe that if we stay out of trouble, do well in school, and pursue a worthy career, we will have achieved the dream, with success and happiness all but inevitable. I believe this to be a half-hearted relative truth, ingrained and imprinted upon us from our youth. We have not been encouraged to explore the soul programming.

We were never really encouraged to ask, who am I? What is it that I have come here to do? How can I truly express what I am within the world where I'm existing? It can feel like we exist in a system designed to sustain blind reliance, compliance, and obedience, fidelity to the status quo – the monotony of it all. If we are ever to thrive beyond this life cycle, we must reconcile with our "soul programming." Soul programming serves as the compass to the unique self "path of authority." Your path of authority is the place of alignment, a point of power that sets you on fire because you are engaged in activity that gives you sweet purpose and satisfaction inside, due to your active alignment with your mission.

Imagine a world free from the pressure of stature by degree, and the measurement of fortune by material wealth, and free from the constant lingering threat of poverty through total loss. The threat of loss glosses the essence of fear over any other programming that is not in compliance with the current system. In this system, the more you gain in the world, the more you lose in your remembrance of the message you came here to share. It reminds me of *The Never-Ending Story II*. In the movie, every time Bastian made a wish with Auryn, he lost a memory that was connected to who he was in the "real world" as a price for his request. The price for your assimilation is to be confined to an identity that's not fully yours. You are working a career that you spent a lifetime creating all for the sake of safety and security in the material world of Pentacles, yet you are restless and unsatisfied because you never questioned if the price of that safety and security aligned with your soul's calling.

If you are reading this book, you believe that there's something within you that feels off; you don't feel quite right; it's discernable by the deep longing within. Despite all that you have achieved thus far, there's something yet for you to do. As a result of this dissatisfaction, you feel unhappy, distressed, depressed, and isolated because now you exist in the awareness that there's something more to your very being, and in this newfound sight, there's partial freedom because you are now unplugging. Now, with your limited awareness that something isn't right, you are no longer a mindless cog in a wheel, but an aware cog. Despite this awareness, you still exist and have to function within the realm and under the authority of the Emperor, exemplified by the many external demands. But what of the demands of the soul trying to lead you to your path of authority?

The soul is the highest and original authority; until now, you have yielded to the default programming focused on the external and illusory, not to the compass of the soul. Lost in the illusory, you feel the longing to exit the game you are currently playing, confused about how to eject from the current monotony. Are you needing Clarity? Check-in with the Higher Consciousness to align with your path of your authority. Check-ins allow you to gain insight and clear understanding of what you must do to come into alignment with your heart's longing. I believe this longing is a language of the soul: the master controller presenting you with the opportunity to reset and take on a new role, a new reality, a new experience where you are now the healer that has been longing for yourself, the healer you were born to be. This reset allows for the unleashing of the divine healer from the restraint and confines of self-doubt, inadequacy, judgment, and fear – all limiting beliefs.

You have always felt a power stirring inside; it's your divine healing light. You have a natural ability to spread the healing balm. This healing energy can express in so many ways; perhaps it's your healing smile, your healing hugs, your healing words, your healing hands, your healing song; there are so many avenues to facilitate and be a conduit for healing. There is a deep knowing that you can help facilitate the physical, mental, emotional, and spiritual healing of those who come into contact with your intentional healing light, and you love the impact that you have on humanity. You feel charged with power and infinite joy every time you extend the light towards your brother and sister; this is the sign of alignment; this is a sign that you are operating in the path of your authority. If not for the financial pressure and social expectation, you could thrive in this state without a care for compensation; you have such resonance, so much so that there's guilt connected with charging because what you generate is priceless, and you could do it for free because walking in the authority of your healing light feels like compensation. Being the light and following the path of the healing call is the key to your perpetual freedom.

Maybe you don't feel confident or secure in your gifts and your ability to work your gift professionally, or you have a confidence in your gifts but have no clue about how to prepare for the journey ahead to becoming a healing practitioner. In either case, you hear the call of the healer, and it has led you to consider The Tarot. Perhaps you had a Tarot reading and thought it was illuminating how the cards mirrored your energy. Now you are curious about how the Tarot can guide your journey to the healing arts; your limited exposure to the Tarot has now opened you to this tool's healing potential and its opportunity for personal and professional development. The ideal reader sees potential in the cards and is open to learning from their wisdom and willing to apply their lessons.

In the course of preparing to write this book, I began to

wonder what it was that I had to say that was so valuable that I would invest the time and effort to produce a work from the depths of my soul. I figured I would speak to and for the people who feel lost in a world that perpetuates constant forgetting; the forgetting of who we are: God-realized, divine beings. I'm speaking for and to the people hoping to experience the sweet awesomeness of their eternity. It takes courage to live in the light of your awesomeness when you live in a dense world where, to use a Tarot image, the Emperor's authority and rigid judgment are a constant threat to true awakening.

This book focuses on the "pre-work," the preparation process, the stage critical for people who don't even know how or where to begin to move into alignment. It will be essential for you to undertake the internal preparation work to begin the transition process. The prework will allow you to embody the healer within and become the healer that will be able to start a business.

I realize some readers may like their current career on some level, but in their current capacity, their gifts are not yet expressed and so they still hear the call for liberation from within. That may or may not mean leaving their job to answer the call.

Perhaps there is an alternative course of action. You can honor the call by starting a part-time business as a healing practitioner offering the Tarot and Reiki – and your healing hugs – to start. The steps in this book will, at the least, get you practicing your gifts with confidence and authority, even if part-time. This process will offer you the opportunity to place deliberate focus on unleashing the healer and to soothe the longing within.

This book will provide insights on how to finally unplug from the monotony and connect with and accept the call of the divine healer within. I will help you commune with your true self, so you can ask and answer the hard and relevant questions and do the essential preparation work critical to unleashing your gifts with confidence. The insights will help you create a healing practice that will invoke a lasting sense of safety and security – a security gained through the freedom of honoring your path of authority as a healer.

Chapter 2

The Journey of a Living Soul

Drawn from Eternity

Eternity Wrapped in the Body

*F*rom the nothing, I was formed, and all that ever was or shall ever be was contained within it. From this space, I became a focused stream of Light, a clear thoughtform manifested in and from the Mind of God, showing up and expressing as Zachary D'jon Weaver. From the stars, I was drawn down to Earth, entering the vessel of my birth, my mother's womb, where I grew in my human expression. It was here where I rested and accepted the shock of transition. The final push was birth, which drew me further from the remembrance of the truth of my original abode – eternity – and entered a perceived disconnection from the all-pervading glory that I was accustomed to. With my first breaths, I let out cries of sadness, and they were thunderous. Only the loving arms of my guides could provide for me a fraction of the comfort I had departed.

Birth was my first experience of separation and practicing the liberation that comes through acceptance. I have come to accept that, in part, my mission in this human existence was to experience loss and then acceptance; and it's through this total acceptance that I would have revealed true wisdom. By this, the healing of the soul would be complete, so that I might experience no more within – that relative human experience of relative loss.

A Child and Different

My journey to the healing arts started far back when I was a child. I was always considered shy, introverted, curious, and inquisitive. I seemed to know stuff and had no clue as to how I knew it. I was a natural at Jeopardy. From a very early age, I could feel energy and had experiences with astral projection. I also could feel the plants and the trees speaking to me. They would give me guidance on what I should do with them ritually to get into a place of peace. Growing up was tough, but nature was always available to nurture me and replenish my soul. While I felt alone and isolated in the physical world with other humans, I never felt alone in the realm of the spirit. Since I can remember, I've always been a conduit. I was very empathic. I could feel everything so deeply. Sometimes it felt like hell on earth. It took me a lifetime to understand that sometimes what I was feeling didn't originate from me and to learn to differentiate.

I was always looking towards Heaven. From my earliest memory, I consulted the stars. I saw freedom in their existence. I always felt that I came from the stars. As a child, I was fascinated with the night sky and always felt a deep desire to return to them. Similar to the Star card in the Tarot, the sky invoked awe, and the feeling that there was a power beyond this world that was responsible for my existence, and that was guiding me and watching over me. I never felt like I truly belonged in this world. I was always seeking to be out of my body. I was always using my imagination; I was always dreaming. To me, my nighttime and daydreams felt closer to reality, and I longed to return. However, for some reason, beyond my conscious understanding, I was here and would have to endure all that would come in the course of life. I had to pay the price of enrollment for living in this dense realm, and I would have to learn to remember the purpose of my attendance through experiences. I would later find out that the price would be accepting all that "I am" – the spirit and the man would have to be joyously unified and perceived as a beautiful and essential part of the whole.

The Hierophant would begin to visit me when I was young. The Hierophant represents my quest for knowledge, a deeper education aligning with the knowing of the spirit. I felt deep within that there was more to my human experience than what was being expressed by conventional religious systems. Frustrated and disenchanted, at the age of fourteen, I embarked on a journey to find "God." I wanted to find God because I was finding it difficult to adjust to the expectations and demands for assimilation. I no longer felt that the teaching I was receiving every Sunday was appropriate for my expansive understanding of the Creator.

My spirit guides would soon direct me to the library. I would spend countless hours in the Harold Washington Library in downtown Chicago, hoping to find the meaning of my existence. I landed in the philosophy section. I was reading books about anything that would give me enlightenment. Some of the first books that attracted my attention related to meditation and energy healing. So did books on how to connect with your guardian angel and spirit guides; how to work with stones and crystals for healing; Feng-shui, psychic ability, the aura, magic, astrology, the Tarot, etcetera.

During this time, the angels would encourage me to not only read the books but to practice. This was when I started my exploration with meditation, so I could hear clear communications from my guides. During one of my practice sessions, my grandmother walked into my room, observing me reading the cards with my candle and incense burning, and she reacted with, "Lord Jesus, he doing voodoo in my house." It is funny to me now, but I guess in a way I was. I say it proudly now because I have nothing but respect and honor for all African religious traditions. My grandmother was a Christian and religious woman, and she loved the Lord; she provided me my foundational understanding of her God, but my soul was seeking a God of my understanding, and my God supported my exploration of esoteric learning and healing modalities.

One Sunday, while attending my grandmother's church, I wore my clear quartz crystal given to me by a Rastafarian elder I met during my quest for knowledge. I was new to using crystals and very happy to learn and practice. When I was approached by an Evangelist in the church who asked me about my crystal, I told her what it was for, and I began to explain with joy and enthusiastic excitement all the properties of a clear quartz crystal. Soon after, she began to chastise and educate me on what the Bible said about the use of this tool. She called it soothsaying, and while I was not yet mature enough to challenge her, she instilled a fear within me (the killer of dreams); she convinced me that God would disapprove of me. I didn't want God to think I was being disobedient and doing the devil's work. She made me trash my charm and warned me to stay away from pendulum and Tarot.

From Child in Pain to Adult Forgiveness

As a child, I spent countless hours in my imagination. It was far better than reality. I felt alone in the world, isolated, different in so many ways. Straight from the womb, I seemed to face a world where my sensitivity was to be a curse. I would get sad often; it was usually about how unfair or mistreated I felt. It was difficult for me as a child, and even at times as an adult, to understand or accept that humans could be so cruel and hurtful to each other. I was bullied a lot growing up. I was never the fighter, always the diplomatic lover. I was very naive, and when forced to fight, I was always the victor, but I was heartbroken because it was against my nature. I was heartbroken because even then I knew that behavior was not in alignment with my soul.

The physical world seemed so cruel, so hard to exist in. It felt like a scary and dangerous place. I didn't feel free to be vulnerable. My level of sensitivity seemed like a blessing and a curse. There was always the chance that I would be hurt or taken advantage of. I experienced feelings of anxiety, feeling trapped in a reality I no longer wanted to experience. I was unfulfilled very early in life, long before I would experience the pain and suffering that come from working on a job that was unfulfilling and monotonous. The earliest pains or traumas that led to unfulfillment were the death of my biological mother, the incarceration of my biological father, and soon after, the death of my maternal grandmother who raised me. Each one, a unique and life-changing event, pushed me closer to the mercy of the Creator.

One of my early opportunities to experience the pain and hurt of loss was the death of my biological mother, Tempia. I can hardly remember her now; she died three days after my tenth birthday. From what I recall, she tried to be a good parent to my younger brother and me, as much as her sick body would allow. Most of my memories of her are of sickness, amputations, and hospitals. As a consequence, my brother and I would never enjoy the privilege of childhood stability. During this time, I was physically abused and sexually assaulted, and as always, it was someone close to the family who would take advantage of this instability. This instability affected me on a mental and emotional level.

Childhood trauma can be complex and difficult to access. I felt unsupported, unseen, and abandoned by my mother. I understand now, as an adult, that sickness can prevent a parent from being an available parent; at the same time, a child needs his mother. Being without her support caused major trauma during my formative years. My mother would miss many of my childhood accomplishments; she would never be the parent that would come to pick up my report card or attend parent-teacher conferences, awards ceremonies, school recitals, or graduations. During those early years of life, I felt very much alone. Some memories, I can hardly recall because they have been suppressed due to the trauma of it all.

I didn't come to terms with my mother's death until I traveled to Peru for an ancient plant medicine ceremony. The goal of the plant medicine experience is to facilitate healing. During my ceremony, my goal was to understand how I could have a stronger connection with my ancestors. I discovered how and got so much more. While communing with the plant medicine, I had an opportunity to experience the cosmic serpent. To me, this was the primordial power revealing itself to me in the form of a serpent. She is kind and gentle, yet she disciplines her children to teach them fully the lessons of the time. When you think she's done with you, she will draw you back. It's as if she possessed me. She moved through me, and I moved like a snake. In this way, she has a sense of humor. She didn't release me until humility, grace, thankfulness, and mercy, among so many attributes, found their way into my heart. She felt like a mother, and she opened my eyes. The channels of the kundalini were open. She rose up from my root chakra to my crown; there was so much energy and information pulsing through me. I was exhausted by the download of information. I asked the serpent to take me to my biological mother, and immediately I was transported to my mother's womb. While I was in her womb, I could feel all my mother's emotions, I could feel all her hopes and dreams, all her desires and prayers for me in this world. It was here where I realize that I harbored years of resentment towards a woman who loved me and wanted so much for me in this world. I would also realize this was the reason for the ancestors' unresponsiveness: I was not ready, because I was not honoring my mother's memory – a link in the blood chain. And this was the truth, I forgot my mother and for this, I felt ashamed and compelled to ask for my mother's forgiveness. The very moment I asked for forgiveness, I purged, I vomited profusely, I was being cleansed.

Aya is a strong medicine. As a result of that experience, my mother and I are closer than the breath. The cosmic mother showed and revealed to me many things. I asked the cosmic mother what my purpose was in this life and she begin to explain that I was to be a healer and the Tarot and the Runes would play a role on the path.

Today I'm filled with humility, reverence, and so much respect for my biological mother and the cosmic mother.

Another opportunity to heal and overcome hurt and abandonment was from my biological father. I only ever met him but a handful of times, and most of those occasions, he was intoxicated. I remember the time his abandonment hit me so strong. My mother was dead at the time, and my grandmother was raising me. My dad had called to speak to me. I honestly had forgotten he existed, but when he called, the longing for a father I never knew grew strong, and I was excited. He said he was on his way to get me. I got dressed and anxiously waited outside on the steps. Seemed like hours went by, and I waited on those steps, excited to welcome the love of a parent. The darker it got, more I realized he was not coming. I could see the pain in my grandmother's eyes because she could feel the pain resting heavy upon my heart. I said to her that day with tears in my eyes, "Don't nobody love me GG," and she said to me, "Baby, I love you, I love you too hard." This I will always remember, and this love forever grounds me.

I didn't see or speak with him again for years at a time. He was incarcerated the majority of my life. It would be years later when I would see him. This was during a time in my life when I was trying to figure out who I was in the world. I suffered from severe depression because I felt lost in the world. I felt that life was harder for me and that if I had a father, life might have been different. But when you do the sincere spiritual work, you come to the understanding that all that has happened was in divine order. I couldn't be the man that I have grown to be if I had not endured all that I have.

To heal, I decided to travel across the country to visit my biological father in prison. I wanted to talk with him with the hope of getting a clear understanding of his perspective. I also wanted to see what he could tell me about my mother from his point of view. The visit was a healing opportunity for me, and I imagine it was an opportunity for him to forgive himself. It was healing all around. Of all his family in all those years, he said I was the only person ever to visit him in prison. I imagine that was difficult for him, having his only son, whom he neglected, find the means within his heart to come and share his healing light with a man he never truly knew. Following that meeting, we maintained some limited contact, but it was nothing consistent. Some years later, he was released from jail, and he died a year later from a heart attack.

My biological father existed no more in this earthen form. His death severed my last remaining biological parental connection in this world. The two physical conduits of my birth have transcended their earthly bodies and have been called forth to rejoin eternity. It was a sad day for me in this realization, but the ancestors whispered, "You are strong," and, indeed, I am.

In truth, even though my dad was an absent parent – I did not have a close relationship or know him as well as I would have liked – I felt something intense within me once he was dead. I used to imagine that on the day of his death, I would feel nothing except for detachment because he was a stranger, but that was an illusion. It was a mixture of numbness and all parts of every emotion. Although he was absent from my life for almost thirty-four years of my existence, a child still longs for the love and security of his father. The fact is he was my dad, and he helped to give me life. And my life is extraordinary and filled with purpose. So, needless to say, I felt loss. I grieved for the man I never knew, the father I never had. I grieved for the child never fully redeemed by the real sincere works of a father. I mourned the end of a possible future that would never be actualized.

When I reflect, in my grief, there is still peace. I found comfort in forgiveness and acceptance, and in that, I believe we both are free from suffering. In the end, it matters not that my dad was absent. His absence revealed in me a strength and a resolve. The ancestral blood that flows through me reminds me that he's still my dad in life and death, and so his spirit must be remembered.

The principle cards I would receive for this experience were Strength and the Two of Cups. These two energies would teach me the importance of exercising compassion and forgiveness. I would have to surrender my ego for the sake of healing and reconciling my relationship with my father. The ancestors further allowed me to understand that for me to honor my ancestors, I must, without reservation, honor the man responsible for contributing his life spark to my existence. I must pay tribute to the blood bond. He must be remembered because of the part he played in the magic of my creation. This trauma – this pain – had to be reconciled for the healer to be healed.

One of my last early childhood traumas that I had to heal from was the death of my maternal grandmother, Mary; I called her GG. She was a southern woman from the Mississippi Delta. She was my first teacher, my rock, my hope, and my first mother. Growing up, I recall when I would act out being a very vibrant child at times, and my grandmother would discipline me. I would say in a tantrum, foolishly, "I'm going to tell my mother." She would respond, "Tell her, I'm your mother's mother. I'm your first mother." She died when I was seventeen. I was finishing my last year of high school during her transition. If it had not been for her love and teachings, my life likely would have been harder than it was.

The pain and trauma of those losses have been life-altering. And have been lessons for my elevation in the healing arts. I am neither my circumstances nor a product of my environment. I am resilient and more magnificent than my trauma. The key to this realization, to this freedom, was and is acceptance of what "is." The acceptance of loss and tragedy have prepared and focused my will on a prosperous and service-driven existence. I believe in the infinite spirit that dwells within you, me, and all of us. This life force has allowed me to write these words of inspiration, a testament to my life's journey. The path has already been laid before me and will continue to reveal itself until fulfilled.

As a result of our trauma, there are times in life when we make mistakes or sin. In spite of ourselves, we let the failures and inadequacies of our humanness overshadow the only Truth that is relevant in this journey. We all experience difficult and dark times. I want you to know that in the darkness, we find illumination. You need only look, commanding the "light" within, shining forth from eternity. In the darkness dwells potential, a silent stirring, waiting to be birthed.

The Fight to Overcome Insecurity

Those early childhood losses were the beginnings of my struggle to overcome the fear of insecurity. I maintained a deep connection with Source energy and my team of guides, and I knew they were looking out for me, making sure I remained alive and well. My growth towards the healing path was delayed because I was distracted, in the sleep of forgetfulness (a state of being where awareness of our power of cocreation is limited by unconscious limiting beliefs and actions), hurled into a fight or flight mode. My focus was just pure survival at the age of seventeen upon the death of my grandmother/mother. However, the path of liberation is inevitable. My focus turned towards a stabilizing opportunity through education. I didn't have a functional nuclear family – my extended biological family was not a reliable or consistent source for healthy growth and security – so my academic studies became my primary focus. I had to make sure I created a secure life, and I knew the only way to secure that future was through having a degree and gaining a career that was suitable to my interests and sustainable.

I went to school for political science and public administration. These fields seemed to interest me. I enjoyed the ideas of government and its structure, and I appreciated the idea of helping to create and implement policy that made a positive difference in the lives of the least of us. So, I pursued a career in government and legislative affairs and criminal justice corrections.

While I'm very grateful for what I have achieved academically, and grateful for my years of service in corrections as a public administrator, I felt like I was missing something.

I was not fulfilled inside, and this missing piece began to get bigger and bigger. My soul sought something more and wanted to have a more immediate and tangible impact on my people; it's as if the soul was calling to me. During this time, I was experiencing increased anxiety about work and my future, personally and professionally. These questions stirred up some hidden emotions. I was trying to figure out how to work out what I needed to be doing. I needed to understand my soul's calling. I felt deep inside that I was called to do more, and I felt it had something to do with the journey I started all those years ago in the library.

It is usually during those painful times that we come to remember our potential, and that was the case for me. Some time ago, I met my mentor and teacher Beverly during a time in my life where I was grieving and trying to transition from a toxic relationship and, at the same time, trying to understand what my next move was personally and professionally. Bev was very supportive. During our connection, she could sense my gifts; it's as if she came to remind me of my potential. She offered me the opportunity to release and let go of the clutter of my past, accept my calling as a divine healer, and to focus my gifts. She provided me a sense of community and a safe space to practice my Tarot reading skills. She taught me about the importance of honoring and trusting my intuition and inner judgment when it came to the interpretation of the Tarot.

Bev was a very affirming figure. She's depicted as the Queen of Swords. She was that wise teacher who had experienced a great deal in life – the good, the bad, and the ugly – but she was not bitter. She was open-hearted and open-handed. If not for her faith and encouragement, my path to the healer within could have been delayed further.

Reading the Tarot came naturally to me. I would often read for myself to check-in, or I would read for others for fun. But I never thought I would be using the Tarot as a tool to heal myself and to facilitate healing for other individuals' transitions. I didn't know this fun tool would support my calling as a healer.

It didn't take long after receiving so much encouragement for me to create my part-time business. I gained the confidence to do this because of supportive people like my colleague Preshelle. She is a Light warrior, and we are bound together in the love we share for our spiritual Mother, Oshun of the Sweet Waters.

Preshelle would say to me, "I see you hiding." It is laughable now. I'm six-two, I have a muscular build, a bald head, and I'm not too bad looking, so how could I be hiding in a room full of people? Well, as it turns out, I was. When I think about it, I was hiding my light. The truth was I was only hiding it from myself because everyone else could see it but me.

Preshelle would often comment on how great I was as a person; she would always remind me that my very existence was a gift and would express how accurate my readings are. She further encouraged me to start my part-time Tarot business. It was not until I began the internal preparation work through the sincere use of the Tarot that I was able to heal myself, accept my calling, embody my authority, and fully honor my path as a healer. As a result of my inner work, I created a part-time business. I created a divinely inspired logo. I created and designed my business website. Not long after that, I started attracting clients and traveling across the country to participate in exposés and festivals. My mission in this life is to help others understand how the Tarot can help them prepare their souls' path as lightworkers.

To live in this corporeal form has been the greatest of sacrifices, but to live righteously in accordance to my highest compass, my Spirit, has made the Fool's Journey satisfying. To live in awareness of the truth of my existence keeps me ever connected to the Master of Above and Below. Resting in this connection brings me in alignment to the Light that I have come to this earth to express. Today, I stand in the perfect wisdom of the Magician within. I bathe in the energy of the Empress of abundance. I dwell beyond the veil of the High Priestess, and I radiate the mighty power of the Sun that is me.

My grandmother always said, "Baby, a half-done job ain't a done job at all." This was usually expressed when I was mopping the floor (and was not committed to the task because I didn't want to do it; I was not committed to its execution or the outcome being perfect). I think this expression is true for healers seeking to be active in the healing arts but not willing to do the foundational healing work to be effective conduits of healing. Well, at this moment, I want to say, the job is well done because if you are reading this book, and you are truly committed to making the effort to connect with your path of alignment, your healing path of authority. Keep reading and stay in the flow.

Chapter 3

A Look at the
Journey Ahead

The following chapters will provide an introduction to the Tarot: what the Tarot is as a divinatory tool and the structure and meaning of the cards. The text will discuss how the Tarot can serve as an instrument for personal and professional development by discussing seven case studies of transformation through honoring the wisdom and insights offered by the Tarot. Further, I will provide the best practices to employ when preparing for the Tarot-reading process. The best practices cover connecting with the spirit guides, selecting a Tarot deck, determining the inquiry, and selecting the most appropriate Tarot spread.

I provide seven insights that are critical to facilitating true healing and transformation. The insights provide a perspective from which to approach the Tarot when seeking to transition into a space of harmony and balance. Adopting and practicing these insights will allow the opportunity for transition and proper alignment with your true path.

The first insight will discuss the importance of *Listening* to the still, small voice of the subconscious mind. In chapter seven, you will get fully enlightened about the Tarot and its ability to serve as a mirror of the soul.

The second insight will discuss the importance of *Accepting* the call. Chapter eight will emphasize the power of acceptance and provide an opportunity to gain a clear understanding of what you need to accept to facilitate the transition.

The third insight will discuss the importance of *Grounding* in the energy of compassion. In chapter nine, you will learn about the transformative power of grounding yourself in the energy of compassion. You will understand what you need to have compassion towards to facilitate transition.

The fourth insight discusses the importance of *Embodying* the authority of self- expression. In chapter ten, you will learn about the nature of your authority and the power of your unique self-expression.

The fifth insight will discuss the importance of *Focusing* the will. Chapter eleven will emphasize the necessity of having clearly defined focus and will guide you towards understanding what your true focus should be at this time.

Chapter twelve discusses the sixth insight, the importance of Trust. It will bring you clarity on how critical it is to have a sincere trust in the Divine Order to facilitate a successful transition.

The seventh insight will discuss the importance of *Releasing* and letting go. In chapter thirteen, you will be introduced to the debilitating effect of holding onto constructs that no longer serve you and will gain a clear understanding of what it is you must release and let go to influence your transition.

In the insight chapters, I have provided seven original Introspective Transition Spreads (ITS) for the reader to explore. Each offers specific clarity about the chapter's insight, unique to the reader. Performing these exercises will allow the reader the opportunity to actually gauge where they are relative to each insight advocated in the text. Once you have an honest view of where you stand energetically, you can better prepare for transition into your healing work with the support of the honest and direct feedback the Tarot provides.

My wish for you is to gain focused confidence though the clarity you will receive about your path by reading this book. Gaining clarity and focus will provide you the compass you need to transition beyond the places of fear that limited your expansion until now. This compass will guide you to a path that is in perfect alignment with the Divine will. These insights will provide the chance for the healer within to be healed, and, in return, to heal the world around you. This book will give you the tools you need to free yourself from the bondage of an unfulfilling existence and unleash the healer within.

Now that we've covered my journey to the Tarot, let's dive further into what is the Tarot exactly.

Chapter 4

What Is Tarot?

*W*ho are we, relative to what there is, within the absolute existence of all things? From where did we come? Why are we here? These are the questions for the ages. There have been many attempts to glean into the truth of "it," and all who dared, expressed only a part of the eternal truth that exists within and around us. Our existence in and of itself is evidence of the boundless possibility brought forth from Source. All life pours from the same vessel, born of pure *de-light*. Our very corporeal form and spiritual nature all converge towards this deep knowing. The Tarot has reaffirmed this deep knowing that God is everywhere present, that energy is always in all places.

Further, that invisible web of energetic interconnectedness intertwines all life. This stream of connectedness serves as a conduit for accessing a universal consciousness, where infinite knowledge exists. This knowledge can be targeted and downloaded. This information download can take place using various divination mediums; Tarot is just one of my preferred tools to communicate with the realm of the eternal.

History of the Tarot

The history of the Tarot and its origins are just as mysterious as the Tarot itself. There are many thoughts on how the Tarot came to be but nothing conclusive. No one truly knows where the cards originated. Some authorities date it back to the recent fourteenth and fifteenth century in Europe, because the earliest known complete deck was found there. Others argue the Tarot dates to the continent Africa and ancient Kemet/Egypt and the mystery schools, which is the most popular theory. The proposition is that Tarot came from Africa and came into Europe in the fourteenth century with nomadic people.

According to scholars, the Tarot deck is a language that only the initiated could understand. The Major Arcana represent the stages of development necessary for initiates as they progress towards the status of adept. The Tarot reflects the evolution of human life experiences.

Tarocchi cards are the ancestors of contemporary Tarot and playing cards and can be traced back to around the late fourteenth and fifteenth century. They were the first sets of playing cards, which were used for games, and featured four different suits. These suits were like what we still use today: wands or clubs, coins or diamonds, cups or hearts, and swords or spades. The original purpose of Tarot was viewed as a social game, not as a divinatory tool. The use of the cards for divination started to become popular in the late sixteenth and early seventeenth century. By the eighteenth century, each card had been assigned specific meanings, and layout options developed for divinatory purposes.

Some of my earliest card game memories are of my grandmother Mary aka GG, my aunt Lorine, and my elder cousins Lisa and Belinda around the dining room table playing Spades. (All have transitioned back to the Source that sustained them; may their memory be a blessing). I would hear laugher, debate, shouts of "you reneged, give me them books," and loud noises of victory as the Ace and the Joker come in to save the day. As a child, I would play "go fish" with my younger cousins. When I got older, I would join the ranks at the adult spades table. I tell you playing cards was a big deal in my family; card games could probably lead to anger and frustration and maybe even some fights. So, you better play well, and you better play to win!

Many people love playing card games yet have no clue that they are playing with a system that came directly from a divinatory language. The modern deck of playing cards is like the grandchild of the Tarot. People love their card games but fear the Tarot. The reality is that every time you pick up a modern deck of cards, you play with remnants of the Tarot, up until now you were just ignorant of the historical connection. For example, the four suits of the minor arcana are almost identical to the modern suites. The names just changed. Card players are familiar with the suit of diamonds. Unbeknownst to them, those diamonds derive from the Tarot suit of pentacles (coins or discs). What about those clubs? Well, in the Tarot, they are called wands (rods or staves). Hearts are cups (goblets, or chalices), and the spades are swords (blades). The Joker is associated with the "Fool" of the major arcana. Fascinating, right? An excellent example of "hidden in plain sight." So, the next time you pick up and play with a deck of cards, please know it relates to the divination system of the Tarot! You can even perform readings with modern playing cards. How cool is that?

A Divination Tool

Tarot is a divinatory tool for healing, transformation, and illumination. It allows you to peer deeply into the mirror of the soul. Its application can allow you to see the underlying energies that surround and affect you in a very real way. This tool provides an opportunity to assess and prepare for what's to come and to set course corrections. I liken Tarot reading to reading computer code; in this case, you are the computer program. The Tarot analyzes and reflects the current program information and predicts the likely outcomes of the program if it keeps running without any modification or intervention.

To explore the world of the Tarot, one only needs to be open and receptive to the experience. Within most cultures, divination exists. There is evidence in the Judeo-Christian tradition of divination. The Bible refers to it as "inquiring of the Lord." The Israelites began to inquire of the Lord many thousands of years ago. They used actual tools like the Urim and Thummim, which were stones the priests used to determine what the Lord's answer was.

The practice of a form of inquiry is not uncommon and found across the lands. Similarly, the Vikings employed Runes, an ancient alphabet for inquiry. Traditional African practices, notably in Ifá and Yoruba traditions, utilized palm nuts and the Opele for inquiry. The Tarot is just one of many tools in a long history of inquiry. These tools are used to identify the causes and solutions to our personal and collective problems with the ultimate goal of restoring harmony and balance.

The Tarot provides space to amend a perceived reality. Our individual and collective lives can change according to our expressed will. The will is reflected by the thoughts, emotions, and actions we express; they are the building blocks of manifestation, programming codes that the universal system of Divine Consciousness recognizes and responds to. They are akin to the codes we input into a computer program. We must trust (indeed know) that the world is responding to the determined will of the Chariot, manifest by focused thoughts, emotions, and actions. All these components, when working together in perfect balance, are the substance that created our physical reality and, indeed, created worlds.

The Card Structure – Major and Minor Arcana

The Tarot has a total of seventy-eight cards, divided into twenty-two Major Arcana and fifty-six Minor Arcana. The twenty-two Major Arcana represent what I call the journey of the living Soul (others refer to it as the Fool's Journey). The cards represent the archetypal qualities that affect humanity on an individual and collective basis. The experiences are represented by characters, like the Emperor and Empress; cosmic forces, like the Star and the Moon; and structures, like the Tower and the Wheel of Fortune. The Major Arcana and some of their meanings are as follows:

0. The Fool: adventure, new beginnings, taking risks
1. The Magician: action, self-control, taking charge
2. The High Priestess: stillness, intuition, wisdom, secrets
3. The Empress: abundance, fertility, resources
4. The Emperor: order, willpower, rules
5. The Hierophant: orthodoxy, education, belief, union
6. The Lovers: love, commitment, beauty
7. The Chariot: emotional control, balance, progress
8. Strength: self-discipline, courage, compassion
9. The Hermit: isolation, inner work, reflection
10. Wheel of Fortune: fate, luck, destiny

11. Justice: fairness, truth, balance
12. The Hanged Man: sacrifice, a new perspective, initiation
13. Death: ending, rebirth, a major change
14. Temperance: patience, moderation, negotiation
15. The Devil: control, codependency, addiction
16. The Tower: sudden change, ruin, breakdown
17. The Star: hope, support, healing
18. The Moon: illusion, secrets, intuition
19. The Sun: happiness, success, growth
20. Judgment: rebirth, second chance, overcoming
21. The World: completion, success, fulfillment

The Minor Arcana are divided into four suits having fourteen cards each associated with an element. The Minor Arcana and some of their meanings are as follows:

- Swords represent the Air element and are associated with thoughts (mind, intellect, and decision).

  1. Ace of Swords: clarity, honesty, truth
  2. Two of Swords: blocks, decisions, balance
  3. Three of Swords: heartbreak, loss, division
  4. Four of Swords: truce, rest, withdrawal
  5. Five of Swords: conflict, defeat, unfair win
  6. Six of Swords: travel, moving away from trouble, recovery
  7. Seven of Swords: avoiding responsibility, deception, scheme
  8. Eights of Swords: restriction, isolation, self-sabotage
  9. Nine of Swords: worry, guilt, overwhelm

10. Ten of Swords: bottoming out, turning point, enlightenment
11. Page of Swords: A person who is ready for action, mental dexterity, a false friend
12. Knight of Swords: A person who is self-assured, impatient, tactless
13. Queen of Swords: A person who is no non-sense, direct, a widow
14. King of Swords: A person who is articulate, direct, wise

- Wands represent the fire element and are associated with desires (creativity, career, and passions).

1. Ace of Wands: initiation, adventure, invention
2. Two of Wands: personal power, courage, establishing something
3. Three of Wands: expansion, foresight, exploration
4. Four of Wands: celebration, freedom, success
5. Five of Wands: competition, conflict, disagreement
6. Six of Wands: victory, pride, accomplishment
7. Seven of Wands: standing up for position, defiance, advantage
8. Eights of Wands: news, quick action, rushing
9. Nine of Wands: sacrifice, defensiveness, alertness
10. Ten of Wands: heavy burden, overwhelm, uphill climb
11. Page of Wands: A person who is ambitious, insightful, confident
12. Knight of Wands: A person who is daring, passionate, enterprising

13. Queen of Wands: A person who is courageous, intuitive, joyful

14. King of Wands: A person who is bold, honest, a powerful leader

- Pentacles represent the earth element and are associated with possessions (the material world, safety, and security).

1. Ace of Pentacles: security, reward, abundance
2. Two of Pentacles: balance, juggling, choice
3. Three of Pentacles: skills, planning, teamwork
4. Four of Pentacles: control, protection, hoarding
5. Five of Pentacles: Total loss, hardship, rejection
6. Six of Pentacles: generosity, consideration, support
7. Seven of Pentacles: evaluation, assessment, inventory
8. Eights of Pentacles: perfecting a craft, practice, diligence
9. Nine of Pentacles: accomplishment, refinement, self-reliance
10. Ten of Pentacles: good life, general wealth, security
11. Page of Pentacles: A person who is practical, focused, realistic
12. Knight of Pentacles: A person who is hardworking, persistent, cautious
13. Queen of Pentacles: A person who is dependable, nurturing, generous
14. King of Pentacles: A person who is reliable, enterprising, supportive

- Cups represent the water element and are associated with feelings (emotions, love, romance).

1. Ace of Cups: love, new romance, fertility
2. Two of Cups: healing, reconciliation, relationship
3. Three of Cups: friendship, celebration, team spirit
4. Four of Cups: self-absorption, introspection, doubt
5. Five of Cups: loss, sadness, regret
6. Six of Cups: nostalgia, innocence, childhood
7. Seven of Cups: wishful thinking, self-indulgence, only one correct choice
8. Eights of Cups: walking away, changing direction, moving on
9. Nine of Cups: wishes fulfilled, satisfaction, pleasure
10. Ten of Cups: happiness, harmony, joy
11. Page of Cups: A person who is sensitive, intimate, romantic
12. Knight of Cups: A person who is emotional, loving, sensitive, artistic
13. Queen of Cups: A person who is empathetic, compassionate, creative
14. King of Cups: A person who is stable, wise, emotionally controlled

The Major Arcana: The Fool's Journey to the Healing Arts

In this section, I walk you through the three lines of seven in the 21 major arcana. The three lines of seven are reflective of the three stages of the Fool's Journey. The first stage represents the outer world, the external challenges to existence in life:

individuality, parental issues, group think, identity pressures, exploring love, creating success, and emotional self-control. The second phase is focused on transformation and the inner world; this is the place where you are tested and perfected by strength, where you gain clarity and a personal compass through the Hermit and Strength. The third phase is about liberation and about being released from the grips of the Devil and freeing yourself from the Tower of old constructs and ways of thinking.

First Line of the Outer World

0.   The Fool: adventure, new beginnings, taking a risk
     The Fool represents your journey to be free from the monotony, the chance to do something different, and your desire to engage in new pursuits. The Fool is the energy of infinite potential before coming into physical manifestation. It's the task of jumping off the cliff without fear or worry. It is an act of soul freedom. It's the act of not letting anything, or anyone, get in the way of the journey ahead. The Fool is the aspiring healer, who takes the chance to explore his or her gifts and abilities without fear of judgment or failure; it's the act of exploring the Tarot as a healing modality and adopting a personal Tarot practice. It is the act of preparing to start a part-time healing practice.

I.   The Magician: action, self-control, taking charge
     The Magician represents creativity and power. The Magician archetype suggests a focused purpose. It's the culmination of the four elements merging

into creative form; the Magician is familiar with the business of creation; he knows how to get things done. The Magician is the healer within; he understands his potential and knows how to actualize that potential in the material world. The Magician is the healer in mastery. He is your conscious aims realized. This energy is the healer educating and supporting all those who come into his or her path. You are the healer coming into alignment with the transformative power of the Magician.

II.   The High Priestess: nonmovement, intuition, wisdom, secrets

The High Priestess is the Healer within that feels stuck. You feel like you are not moving, and you seek the face of God for guidance. You feel a sense of stagnation, and this archetype encourages you to submit to the stillness and surrender to the wisdom of Source's energy. Surrender to Divine Consciousness, where you will find sacred knowledge. The High Priestess is honored by prayer and meditation in a healing practice. The High Priestess speaks to the healer within with words of wisdom. She says to trust your intuition and let it guide you.

III. The Empress: abundance, fertility, resources

A healthy alignment reflects the Empress energy. The Empress represents your passion, love, and overall feeling of abundance. The Empress is the aspiring healing practitioner who loves her work; this is the fullness that comes from working in your path of authority. You exist in the knowledge that you are abundant in your healing gift and your gift brings economic value. In this alignment, there is great pleasure and satisfaction.

IV.   The Emperor: order, willpower, stability
The Emperor represents rules, order, structure, in society. The Emperor provides authority. He knows what's right and has a lot of responsibility for his domain. He's the boss. The Emperor is about taking charge of your life and defending something important. You are taking charge of your life; you are defending your soul's calling to be a healing practitioner.

V.   The Hierophant: orthodoxy, education, belief, union
The Hierophant speaks to your desire of wanting to be released from the bonds of conformity and social expectations. It speaks to your desire within to teach that which is holy and helpful. This energy wants you to learn and teach a craft related to health and spiritual education.

VI.   The Lovers: love, commitment, beauty
The Lovers card speaks to relationship, love, and choice. The archetype reflects the rational and emotional, existing in a harmonious relationship. It's about choosing to follow and act upon what you love. The archetype is about staying true to yourself and going by your very own standards. In the context of

the aspiring healing practitioner, it is about seeking union with the soul.

VII. The Chariot: emotional control, balance, progress
The Chariot reflects your will power and your ability to succeed. You maintain a calm. It's your coming of age. Your ability has mastered your inner world. You have achieved emotional control. The chariot is the healer in motion. You are confident and in control of yourself and ready to charge towards a successful healing practice.

Second Line of the Inner World of Transformation

VIII. Strength: self-discipline, courage, compassion
The Strength archetype reflects strength, patience, and self-control. This energy is about taming the beast within; it's about not yielding to primal animal instinct. It's about being strong enough to show mercy and grace. Strength energy always bestows compassion and love. This energy suggests that you must be kind and exercise patience and compassion when you are an active practitioner of the healing arts.

IX. The Hermit: isolation, inner work, reflection
The Hermit speaks to your quest for illumination and transformation of the self. He must come out from among them; he must travel alone, up the mountain or into the valley for introspection and self-reflection. This inner work is required for the Hermit to find his light and open the doors of transformation. The Hermit

speaks to your searching for direction as you seek to understand how the Tarot can help you transition into the healing arts. It also speaks to your ability to offer guidance and wise counsel as a healing practitioner.

X.   Wheel of Fortune: fate, luck, destiny
The Wheel of Fortune speaks to destiny and the ever-changing movement of life. It's about understanding that everything is working out for you. The archetype indicates a turnaround in life for the better. When you draw this card, you may be unfulfilled in your current capacity, but now that the Wheel of Fortune is here, you can be swept up in new and positive developments. You can get involved in activities that make you feel like the luckiest person alive.

XI.   Justice: fairness, truth, balance
The Justice major arcana is about trust, responsibility, and fairness. This archetype tells us to be fair and honest and to always do what is right. It's also about making decisions from a balanced perspective. From the perspective of the healer in transition, this is you acknowledging your calling to the healing arts. It's taking fair and measured action towards this end. It's about achieving balance through alignment.

XII.   The Hanged Man: sacrifice, a new perspective, initiation
The Hanged Man is an archetype of letting go and sacrifice. It's about surrendering for the sake of getting

what you want. Sometimes that surrender constitutes a matter of perspective, causing you to see things from a different perspective as you hang upside down from Odin's tree. It's about you as a healer in transition, pausing to reflect to begin to see the world and your existence in it from a new angle.

XIII. Death: ending, rebirth, a major change
The Death archetype is about the ending of a cycle and the beginning of something new. It's about transition by eliminating what is no longer serving you. In the case of the aspiring healing practitioner, this growth could be in the form of courage and confidence with the elimination of fear. This Death card could also show up for the intense calling to practice the healing art; when this calling is expressed by Death, this calling is inescapable and can't be avoided.

XIV. Temperance: patience, moderation, negotiation
Temperance is an archetype embodying the energy of compromise, moderation, and balance. Temperance speaks to harmonious relations. It's about channeling the higher consciousness to see the other side. It's about being open, receptive, and in the judgment-free zone. In the context of the healer, I believe synthesis to be the goal; you are trying to find the right combination to flourish and experience wellbeing.

Third Line of Liberation

XV. The Devil: control, codependency, addiction

The Devil represents bondage, hopelessness, and materialism. It speaks to the need for something unhealthy and toxic; it can come across like an addiction. The Devil is a low-level vibration. The Devil shows itself when you allow yourself to be controlled by accepting an unwanted situation. The aspiring healing practitioner can experience this Devil when they continue to exist in a profession, knowing it is not good for the edification of the soul. The Devil shows up when the aspiring healer has self-doubt and a lack of faith in a better future where there is alignment with the call of the healing practitioner. The Devil shows up when you forget the spiritual aspect and only focus on the physical.

XVI. The Tower: sudden change, ruin, breakdown

The Tower is indicative of change, release, and revelation. The Tower comes to say, "What you have built is now destroyed." Things will no longer be as they were. It's the energy of overall upheaval. The Tower is the healing practitioner who has left their old way of thinking, and now they maintain new realizations as a result of the sudden and illuminating truth.

XVII. The Star: hope, support, healing

> The Star card is the energy of hopefulness, generosity, and inspiration. The Star says to have faith and always remain positive and in the flow. The Star offers inspiration for the journey. The healing practitioner must always heal from a place of hope. The Star will help you relax and have peace of mind.

XVIII. The Moon: illusion, secrets, intuition

> The Moon is indicative of fear, illusion, and confusion. The Moon says that you do not see things clearly. As a result of your inability to see, you are engulfed by fear. You fear that you may be wrong in failing the healer's call. You fear that you are mistaken in following the siren's call. You fear what awaits you if you choose wrong, and you fear what awaits you if you choose not to choose. When the Moon archetype appears in a Tarot reading, it asks the question, "Of what am I afraid?" The Moon provides an opportunity for the aspiring healing practitioner to name the fears that are holding you back from the healing arts. Once you identify the limiting belief, you can have a better understanding of what ways of thinking and feeling have limited your actions up until this point.

XIX. The Sun: happiness, success, growth

> The Sun is reflective of enlightenment and greatness. This is where you make sense of all the chaos; it's about the elevation of the truth. This is where the aspiring healing practitioner embodies the healer within. From

the place of the Sun, the practitioner feels free and expansive and exudes enthusiasm.

XX. Judgment: rebirth, second chance, overcoming
Judgment speaks to releasing guilt and sorrow; it's your understanding of what truly makes you happy; it speaks to an inner calling, and your ability to make decisions, without the feelings of regret. It's the monotonous worker, recognizing their true vocation; it's the longing to act on only things that will support your alignment and mutual progress.

XXI. The World: completion, success, fulfillment
The World speaks to integration, fulfillment, and accomplishment; it's about achieving balance and wholeness. View this as the calling being actualized in the physical world in the form of practice. This is about allowing that practice to give you pleasure and peace of mind because you are now in alignment. You have finally realized your heart's desire and are flourishing and prospering in your healing craft.

Now that we've covered the basics of the Tarot and its archetypes, let's dive further into how you can use the Tarot with your transition.

Chapter 5

How Can Tarot Assist with Transition?

Tarot and Two Healing Practices

A "healing practice" can be defined in two ways, and both must be nurtured for the healer to become the healing practitioner they are longing to express. Healing practitioners must be committed to practices for both personal and professional development.

A personal healing practice is the internal work, focused on the healer's own healing. It's the consistent and daily work of perfecting the healer so that there is perfect alignment with their path of authority. (The path of authority is the place of calm and assuredness, where the execution of your efforts is effortless and full of bliss because those executions align with your highest calling).

A professional healing practice is the external work, focused on the "worlds" (we are worlds within a world, surrounded by worlds) around you, serving as a conduit for transmitting healing light, the goal being to support the healing of your neighbor seekers from your seat of authority.

Each practice can be guided with the support of the Tarot.

The Tarot can be an excellent healing modality to employ for personal development. It's also an excellent tool to employ with clients when starting business as an energy healing practitioner. It's a creative tool that will allow your clients to take an active role in their healing. I describe it as a collaborative process. While you, as the healer, facilitate healing and can read the energies that are showing up, it's up to the querent (the person receiving the reading), to be honest about if there is resonance. The key is always to be open and receptive when approaching the Tarot. It's similar to what my Pops, Francis Priester, would say, "Son, you have to be honest with yourself so that you can be honest with God, and then you can be honest with others." Honesty is key, and the root of this is being able to be vulnerable in the face of truth. When viewed from this place, you accept the power of being able to influence and change the *What Is* before you by the guidance you receive, actualized by the power of your will. The Tarot is strong medicine when you allow it to do its perfect work and an invaluable tool in the hands of a practitioner walking in their path of authority.

Tarot: A Tool for Personal and Professional Healing Practice

The Tarot helps you transition from relationship challenges and career challenges, and helps you heal from the deep emotional blocks that hold you back in life. The Tarot can serve as an instrument for personal and professional development. The Tarot allows you to inquire about specific, real-life situations. We all have real-life challenges that we have to address. However, some are more difficult than others. The Tarot can assist you in making the right decision or give insight into why you made such a horrible decision in the first place. The Tarot can reveal your insecurities and pain bodies, offering illumination that leaves you better informed when making future decisions. This tool offers you the opportunity to heal from known hurt and trauma, and from the things that you never realized were holding you back. The Tarot helps you understand if you are on your path, it lets you see how far off the path you are, it lets you see what's getting in the way and the work that must be addressed to be successful in reaching a goal. Or it tells you why you will fail in a goal. It is always illuminating.

For the guidance received from the Tarot to truly work and be effective for transformation, you must listen, which means being open and receptive:

> Release what's no longer serving you.
> Accept what the cards are expressing.
> Ground yourself in the love of God.
> Focus on what you want to manifest, and
> Trust in your power as a co-creator.

The Tarot serves as a mirror, and the reflection is undeniable – well, you can try to deny, but what's the point? I will give you a good example: let's take relationships. My former client Frank was head over heels with a man who he knew for about six months. During their courtship, he realized his newfound love was becoming inattentive and didn't spend much quality time with him anymore. This was hurtful to Frank, but despite the withdrawal, he remained head over heels with this person. He would eventually confront his partner, and the person would be whispering sweet words of love and provide temporary affection to him to calm his hurting, confused, and frustrated heart. When the pain became too great, eventually, Frank consulted me for a reading because he was confused and needed clarity and direction. He came to me because he wanted to know how the relationship would progress. During the reading, I expressed to him that his partner was distracted and avoiding the responsibility of a relationship. I told him he was most likely being unfaithful indicated by the Seven of Swords. I saw that he was being false and deceptive with his words indicated by the Page of Swords, and that the relationship was not going to progress healthily and that it would soon come to a crashing end, indicated by the Tower and Death Cards. I assured him the evidence of this would be revealed to him in short order. This was supported by the Three of Swords. He needed to be ready to accept the truth.

Now, of course, this was very painful for him to hear, but I think he felt this was true. Tarot usually reinforces or confirms what we already know to be true in our hearts. After the reading, Frank would soon learn that his partner had already been in a five-year relationship with another person, well before he met Frank. I advised him on the internal work that he needed to do to help him heal and transition to a space of harmony and balance within himself. Frank became so invested in this work that he began to learn the Tarot so that he could incorporate it into his daily practice so he could check in on his progress. He seemed to be progressing fairly well until the man that hurt him came back around with the desire to try to reconcile with him. He did perform a reading for himself, and it seemed unclear to him, even though the cards were right in his face, telling him as clear as day that a reconnection was not going to be beneficial to him. The truth is he just wanted a different result. So, he consulted me again for guidance. I could see in his mind he was open to giving him another opportunity. He expressed to me his thinking, "Well, we have been down this road before, and my ex realizes how much he hurt me with the lie and the deception. He won't do it again. To hurt me again would be evil," and he didn't want to believe that the man was evil. Well, we did a reading and, I saw hurt, loss, and betrayal. But he was so convinced that this time he would not hurt him, even with the mirror before him, that he just had to try. He tried, and, in the end, not two weeks later, the man betrayed him again.

Frank learned to listen and trust in the Tarot and in his practice with the Tarot; he has become a faithful student of the Tarot; he trusts and honors the guidance it provides. This tool helped him make the life changes necessary for his growth and personal development. The key is to listen and trust in what's revealed to you.

On that note, I need to share a story about my own personal healing through Tarot – the story about me and my brother. Our relationship was challenged. I was very much the Emperor in that relationship, but that was not going so well. You see, the Emperor knows best, and you need to listen and do exactly as he commands. As well-intentioned as this authority is, it can be very imposing, controlling, and off-putting when in excess. Needless to say, that energy caused a lot of tension. The cards were telling me that I didn't know it all and that I had to exercise a great deal of temperance. I mean, the Temperance Major Arcana would come up almost always when it came to our relationship. I would begin to see the number fourteen everywhere, to remind me of how important it was to cultivate this energy. I would ignore the signs, and the tension and conflict would get worse, and worse, as indicated by the Five of Wands.

It got to the point where our issues began to affect my sight, and my healing light. I was not as intuitive as I had been, and I was totally out of the flow, and I was unhappy as a result. I didn't like how far I fell from the light, so I decided to listen to the Tarot and be obedient to the guidance. So now, our relationship is grounded in the energy of compassionate love for each other. I exercise calm, patience, and compassion, as reflected in the Strength and Temperance Cards.

Honoring this tool has allowed my personal and professional life to transition into a state of balance, and my light is stronger as a result. As a result, I don't have any stress or conflict in that relationship; it's healthy and growing. What I am saying is, if you accept the guidance and trust in the process, you can have the life that you truly want.

I had a client named Allision, who was estranged from her mother; they had not spoken in years due to family drama that involves a family secret. Her mother never told her that her father was not her biological father. This was understandably a shock to her system. The only father she had ever known was not the man that gave life to her, and at twenty-five years of age, she was finding this out. Allision loved her mother, but she was hurt, she felt her mother lied to her all of her life. As a result, she stopped talking to her mother. She didn't know how to deal with what she saw as deception, and secrets. Admittedly there were times over the years that she wanted to reconnect with her mother so that she could get more answers, but her ego prevented this healing process.

Now, this client didn't initially seek my guidance on how to transition past this issue with her mother. She came to me regarding her business; she wanted to understand how she could grow in her spiritual gift and grow her business. During the reading, guess what the first thing that came up to her surprise was – the unresolved issues with her mother. Spirit, through the Tarot, was communicating what needed to be healed for her gift to flow and for her business to prosper. This is a good reminder that Tarot may not always address the question you ask in the way you think it might, but it will always address the most pressing need that you may be oblivious to. The underlying issue revealed the key to her liberation. So, the querent should always be open and receptive. The client did the work and reconciled with her mother, and now she is in alignment with her relationships and prospering in her healing gifts, healing the world through the example of her healing.

Tarot is an effective tool with helping transition professionally from a career that's no longer serving you by allowing you to see what's holding you back. My former client Margie was working a job where she was feeling unvalued, and she felt like she was not thriving in her purpose in her current workplace. She came to me because she wanted to know if she should stay or if she should go. The Tarot showed me all the feelings she had surrounding her employment, and they were nothing nice. She felt trapped, unhappy – the woman was miserable. But she asked me if she should stay or go, quite curious. There's always something deeper that keeps a person bound and from not reaching their fullest potential. In her case, the underlying issue was the dream killer, fear. She was afraid to jump ship. At the same time that she wanted to be free from her employer, she was afraid to let go of the security that she had grown accustomed to, even though the price of that security was misery.

During the reading, we discovered her financial insecurity and why she was so fearful. The reading also showed her that she needed to have the courage to jump and needed to have a confident strength in her ability to make it to the other side. The fact was that it was possible to get to the other side. The Tarot provided insights on how she could overcome and do just that. The reading also revealed the price of doing nothing and the reward for following her calling. At the end of the reading, we saw cards reflecting her potential success, rebirth, and a feeling of adventure and freedom. Margie followed the guidance and found the courage she needed to focus her will towards the reality that she wanted for herself. She found the courage she needed to make a move. I call it focusing the will and trusting. Now she's free and has started a consulting firm where she's the boss.

Sometimes I will get a client who is difficult to read for. The challenge is not as a result of my skills with the cards, but the issue lies with the querent's ability to be open and honest. I had a client recently who came to me for a general reading. I began to pull the cards for her, and I began to share with her what I felt spirit was trying to communicate to her. She felt like nothing was resonating with her. He energy felt blocked and pessimistic; she was one of those "prove to me you are real" type of clients, and if you are not confident in your authority, it can cause you to feel insecure in your sight.

Because she expressed the cards didn't resonate, I began to do another spread with a different set of cards, and the same cards proceeded to come up. She was reluctant to agree to any of the interpretations I was giving her, and she was not very forthcoming, but I was determined to stand my ground. I was like the Seven of Wands in the Tarot, an energy representing standing up for your beliefs, defending your position, standing up for what you know to be true, and for that, you will never have any regret. I shared my healing light with her for over an hour to get her to be open to the possibility that what was coming up had some validity; it was only toward the end of the call that she began to acknowledge the truth of what was being revealed.

I'm expressing this case to you so that you don't fall into the trap of doubting the information that spirit presents to you. If you are not confident in your abilities and the information that reveals to you, if you don't stand firm in the wisdom revealed, others' denial of their truth can cause you to feel insecure and challenge the authority you bring to the healing table. Remember that the cards are a tool to be utilized by both you and the client.

The key here is to listen to the guidance, release all issues that the cards are telling you must go. Accept that there is another path for you. Ground yourself for the journey ahead, in the love of God that abides within, and it will give you the strength as you travel the Journey of the Living Soul (the Fool's Journey), embodying your authority with all the experience that you have gathered to date, and with a focused and determined will, create the life that you desire, and trust that it will come to pass.

Chapter 6

How to Read the Tarot

*I*n preparation for your inquiry, it is important to establish some foundational best practices. First is grounding and connecting with your guides, what I call "your team." You do this by requesting their help through prayer and meditation. If you have a great imagination, this is the perfect time to explore that treasure. After you make contact, select the deck, and determine the inquiry, it's time to select the spread appropriate for the question. After that, interpreting the cards is a matter of understanding each principal card's meaning and trusting the guidance the intuitive mind gives to you as you view the selected cards. Remembering to trust is paramount.

Connecting with the Guides

When preparing for a Tarot reading, or any form of divination, it is important to perform essential grounding work, allowing for easier connection with your guides, so they can assist by providing you answers through the tool. I call the guides "your team," assembled to assist you with navigating through the human experience. Members of your team can consist of your spirit guides, angels, ancestors (egun), Nature spirits (the Orisha), the gods, among others.

These benevolent beings exist on higher planes of existence.

They communicate with us in different ways. Some speak to you in your dreams; others speak to you in number sequences or symbols. One of the ways my guides personally speak to me is through the TV and radio. The more sensitive you are, the more likely you will be able to hear, see, or feel their energy around you. For example, I might hear something on the television at the most perfect of times, and you know it was not a coincidence – it was God speaking. Sometimes my deceased grandmother will leave me pennies or I will smell her perfume. In a way, she speaks to me all the time in the form of her teaching. I'm always quoting something she said, so much so I should write a book called *My Grandmother Said*. The point here is when you invite their presence and support, it's important to pay attention and honor the signs.

The best way to begin to establish these connections is by using your greatest creative power, the imagination. When you imagine, you send a signal out to the universe that says, "This is what's possible, and I'm unafraid." To give it momentum, you charge the image with a feeling state. This is a "generator," an emotion – gratitude is always a good one to get you off the ground. The memory of my grandmother and her deep abiding love is an automatic generator for me. You have to identify your creation generator. This is where the thought-idea meets with the passion-filled emotions allowing for manifestation; the goal is to manifest your guides.

Prayer and Meditation

Prayer is the foundational element for making contact with our guides. We must always believe that we are being supported and guided; however, it is just as important to invite their presence actively. We must honor these energies by calling them forth, believing in our hearts that we have gathered the support needed for the task. The key is always to be open and receptive. When I pray, I call upon my ancestors to be with me and to help me to interpret those cards. Also, I call upon the Gods of my African lineage, I call upon my mothers, the sisters three Osun, Oya, and Yemaya to aid with my sight. I call upon Elegua to open the paths to help me to pierce the veil. And I call upon Jesus, the God of my grandmother.

This is my way, but there are many ways. There's only one Source and one Power in the universe and that Source expresses in a multitude of different ways. So, when it comes to prayer, the only rule is that you call out to the God of your understanding to make your request known. All messages lead to the one Source. Prayer opens the gateway, a portal of endless possibilities; prayer matches with faith, and faith opens the door of creation. So, pray for sight, pray for clarity, pray for understanding, pray to be used, pray to be an instrument – a vessel of service. Pray with all humility in your heart and believe your request has been heard and answered.

Now that we have sent out the prayer request, you must practice being open to hearing the word of God when it speaks to you, and the best way to getting in the receptive mode is through meditation. Meditation is said to be conscious sleep; it's a space where you can access the eternal. It's the place where the mind of God is available to you. Meditation takes commitment and sincere effort. You have to let go and be still, trusting in the guidance that is brought to you. Meditation is a state where you become the observer. In this state, you realize that you are more than just the body, and you realize there is something far great than the "you" that is the body. From this state of awareness, you will be able to travel the endless realities and download the infinite knowledge that is available to us as spiritual beings. Meditation calms the chatter of the mind and allows you to make room for the stillness to rise and speak.

Selecting a Deck

When it comes to Tarot, the tradition is that your first deck should be gifted to you. Well, that's cool and all, but if you are anything like me, you can't wait. I will say that it is typical for beginners to start with the Rider-Waite-Smith deck – it's the standard, and most decks that have been created have used this deck as their foundation. I would recommend beginners use this deck to learn and get their feet wet. Otherwise, I would suggest you let your intuitive nudge help you identify the correct deck for you. Trust your gut. It will never lead you astray if you are listening and trusting.

Determine the Inquiry

After you have done your grounding work and selected a deck, now is the time to make the inquiry. The inquiry is the question that you desire to ask. I would recommend you avoid yes-or-no questions. And be as specific as possible. The more specific, the clearer the answers will be. Once you have formed your question, repeat it as many times as you need to have it clear in your mind's eye and heart. As you do this, you will shuffle the deck, and you will shuffle as many times as necessary until you are comfortable. Once you are satisfied, then you cut the cards in three piles, and you pick up the first pile, starting with the center pile and then moving from the right to the left pile. Next, you place the cards down according to the spread that you have identified.

The technique I outlined is my system of reading and does not allow the querent to touch the cards personally. I have at times requested that the querent blow on the cards to allow their energy to penetrate the cards further but that's not always possible when conducting remote reading. However, as you grow in your Tarot practice, you will create and follow your own practice. I know readers who require that the client do all the touching. That is not my system, but you never know, you might find that model works for you. Try them both and see what feels right, in the end, as always, following your inner guidance – the still, small voice – to show you your path in the Tarot.

Selecting a Spread

The selection of a card spread depends on the reader's preferences, skill level with the cards, and the nature of the questions involved; there are hundreds of types of spreads that can be employed during a reading. The most popular, however, are:

> One-card spread,
> Three-card spread, representing past, present, and
> future,
> Five-card spread, and
> Ten-card Celtic cross with at least two versions.

You can even make your own spreads, like I did for this book. So, you need not worry about which spread you will use at this point because I have provided you seven spreads to work from during your personal readings. You will find them at the end of each of the insight chapters. If you want to explore other spreads, make your reading easier by selecting a spread that aligns with the topic of inquiry; it provides more clarity and allows the reader to focus, and clear focus leads to a successful reading.

Now that we've covered the basics on how to prepare for reading the Tarot, let's dive into the seven insights and their corresponding Tarot spreads.

Chapter 7

Listen to the Higher Consciousness

Insights from the High Priestess

If you are reading this book, I can bet that you are or have been experiencing sleepless nights and feelings of restlessness. You may feel a deep longing for something, something you can't even express yet into human words, but undeniably there's something gnawing on the inside, deep within. The longing is for something more, something greater than your current existence. Those are intuitive nudges calling to you in subtle and not so subtle ways.

What if I told you this was, in a way, a language: the language of the subconscious, the higher mind. The subconscious is defined as part of the mind which one is not fully aware of, but which influences one's actions and feelings. I call it the underworld, and it is alive and very influential, making up ninety percent of our minds' function. It's uncharted territory; the other ten percent belongs to the conscious mind. The conscience mind seems pretty important and yet it's insignificant in the grand scheme of things.

I like to look at this from the perspective of the element or the suit in the Tarot or from the lenses of gender. The conscious mind is masculine energy, associated with the suits of wands (corresponding to Fire) and swords (corresponding to Air). These suits hold active energy concerning will power, short term memory, logical thinking, and critical thinking. The subconscious feminine, associated with Cups (representing Water), corresponds with our beliefs, emotions, and feelings, habits, values, protective reaction, long-term memory, imagination, intuition, and creativity. The subconscious mind is the key to unlock that which you are longing to express in this human experience. It is an access point to the higher self, the soul.

What if I told you that among other amazing aspects, a magical element of the Tarot is a mirror into the subconscious mind? It's a door to the true self. The Tarot has the unique ability to reflect your deepest truth, a truth that you either never realized or tried to hide away because it was too difficult to face. The Tarot brings illumination into the darkness. It's like the sun shining high on a bright day; if you are open and receptive, it can glimpse into your soul.

The High Priestess Speaks

I had a client named Eric. He felt stuck in his career as an educator; in his current employment, he felt like he had plateaued. He felt unappreciated and unvalued. He didn't see any opportunity to advance in his career, so he decided to pursue a new faculty position at another institution. He had great hopes of securing the opportunity because he had an inside lead – his mentor was the chair of the department – and he was convinced that he had people on the inside rooting for him, so he knew he would be considered as a serious candidate for the position.

After the interview, the interview panel gave him glowing remarks, including his previous professor, with whom he had developed a mentoring relationship. Several weeks passed, and he had not heard a word about his candidacy, and his mentor stopped returning his email inquiries. Eric came to me with the hope of understanding what was happening in his life professionally and how he could transition from this rut. He wanted to leave his current situation right away because the leadership was causing him some stress. I consulted the cards, and they cautioned him about moving. As the expression goes, the grass is not always greener on the other side. I cautioned him to remain at his position and wait like the hangman with patience because soon his desire for advancement would be realized within the organization.

Sometimes the Tarot advises us to stay put and be still with patience like the High Priestess. This means don't move. The cards also warned that the new prospect he was pursuing was not all it appeared to be as suggested by the Moon Major Arcana, and the Page of Swords indicated a false person, someone not sincere and not telling you the truth.

Weeks later, my client expressed that the job he thought he was a shoo-in for was not going to be realized. As I predicted and he further indicated, the person who he felt was a mentor hired someone else, despite the sweet words to his face. To his surprise, his current job offered him a promotion into the leadership team because some of the senior leadership was retiring.

I use this example to say that it's important to listen to the

Tarot, release what you think you want in the face of what is being presented to you, and trust that everything will work out. Well, it sounds to me like everything worked out, he's better off, and more the wiser.

The Deepest of Searching

Tarot is a tool for illumination and transformation; it brings to light what's hidden beneath. It's very similar to that illustration of the iceberg: the visible tip of the iceberg is nothing compared to the unseen base of the ice, of which no one can know the scope and size with the natural eye. The Tarot is inviting you to go deeper. In that deep, sight becomes clear, and the profound and honest searching can begin.

I recall a time when I was suffering from feelings of deep hopelessness. Frankly, I was a big emotional mess. I'm a Pisces, so having a vast array of simultaneous emotions, that can't be cohesively explained, is not unusual. However, those feelings can become unbearable because it can be challenging to readily give shape in words to the rhyme or reason for my dis-ease.

I didn't know what I was feeling or how to express the lingering and subtle emotions. The thoughts were not perfectly identifiable within me. My internal compass was off. I was like a ship lost at sea, drifting upon the deep waters, wandering, but far within, desiring salvation from the endless voyage of monotonous existence. In this state of being, one can feel like a vessel without a destination, sailing in a fog of uncertain direction. Time itself seems to move slowly around you, and you are keenly aware of its presence. This limited awareness further perpetuated the agony of this state of existence, confirmed by the guttural expressions of spirit: agony, borne out of the longing for something far more profound and soul-enriching.

It was during these moments of awareness that I found myself searching intently for the force that was responsible for my existence. I was searching for the source of all there is, deeply desiring an audience with the Master. I desired to bare my soul, and present my inquiries, with the hope of bringing me closer to the closure of my meaning, a meaning that had long escaped me. This world seemed to me like a barren land, full of illusions, shadows on a rocky surface. Yet, beneath her mantle were the wellsprings of life.

Beneath is where we must surrender all. In surrendering, we create the gateway that leads one from the barren land to the wellsprings of eternity.

The Tarot is one of the most profound tools for accessing what's beneath. When I turned to Tarot, for insight about the future direction of a volatile and toxic relationship with a former partner, I gained a clear understanding of my heart's desires, challenges, and emotional state, all perfectly laid before me. The only task at the time was to be honest and accept what spirit presented to me.

The Tarot opens the door to the intuitive mind. I have learned to trust the still, small voice. Trusting the subconscious mind, and the insight it brings to you, is another key to your liberations.

However, the act of listening is not enough; you must also accept and act upon the revelations. Acting is a sign of trusting. When you trust in the spirit that dwells within, coming to you via the subconscious mind, you will never go wrong. The subconscious has all the answers and solutions to all your issues of the day. That job or situation that no longer serves you? The subconscious truly knows why and has been trying to bring your attention to the perfect solution.

I looked at this through the lens of the High Priestess and the Moon Major Arcana of the Tarot. Both represent that which is not seen with the naked eye. But they both speak to greater awareness, a deep wellspring of infinite knowledge and trust. The High Priestess speaks to us about being still; she tells us to meditate, to seek what's beyond the veil of the physical world for answers. She speaks to us of intuition and the still, small voice. The Moon represents that which is hidden or not clear. The moonlight provides another form of sight, much different than the direct light of the sun, but still reflecting the light of the sun, allowing the unseen to appear. This is the way of the Tarot: it removes all the illusion, and the mirage, presenting what is true before you. It is the clearest of mirrors I've seen thus far, no Windex required.

Trusting the subconscious mind is an essential ingredient for your healing and transformation and a major component in facilitating any form of transformation and transition. The Tarot is the mightiest of mirrors, serving as a reflection of your deeper self. Trust what you feel and be open to the lessons that are readily before you.

Today, you intentionally observe and feel every aspect of your life situation. You ask yourself, "What the insight is here? What am I to gain from this experience? How is this experience serving my highest good?" You will grow stronger and further awaken into your true-self by understanding the power of the indwelling spirit that speaks to you in the still, small voice. At this time, you may be clear on what the conscious mind is saying: you want to be free from that unfulfilling career, free to unleash the healer within you, free from that rut and stagnation, but you don't know how. The High Priestess, and the Moon within, know the how and why. Have trust in your heart when you stand before the mirror to receive her wisdom and accept what's given.

I've provided a Tarot spread so you can explore what lies beneath your underworld. Dear one, what is the still, small voice trying to express to you as you transition towards the healing path? What is it that you need to *hear*?

Tarot Spread: Introduction of the High Priestess

The objective of the four-card "Listening" spread is to provide the querent with the opportunity to gain clarity about the existing impediments to inner listening. The High Priestess serves as the dedicated significator card, a touchstone that adds meaning to the spread. This Major Arcana was chosen to represent your desire and sincere request to receive guidance from the High Priestess, the guardian of that which is unknown, unseen, unspoken, and of the realm of the spirit where infinite knowledge exists. The Tarot spread asks the following:

1. *What impedes my hearing and keeps me from being in the receptive mode?*
2. *What is the message from the Higher Consciousness that I have not been hearing?*
3. *What's the lesson or insight to be gained?*

Figure 1: The Listening Spread

Preparing to Hear the Still, Small Voice of the High Priestess

Invocation to the High Priestess

As you begin your journey to connect and attune to the energy of the High Priestess, it's essential to create space to receive her insights. The initial step is the prayer of invocation. This is the point where you call upon the God of your understanding to intervene and come to your aid. The following prayer should be done before your meditation exercise and the drawing of cards. The ritual of prayer sets an intention and invites your team (your own personal set of guides) to assist you as you attempt to connect deeper to the Source that permeates all. Repeat the following prayer or replace with one that resonates with you more.

> *Into the void, I call to thee – into the spaces where dwells eternity. I invoke the power of the ancient of days, resting on her throne where the crescent moon wains. High Priestess, I call to thee. I seek your divine wisdom; I seek your sacred whisper. Speak to me from beyond the veil. Increase my hearing and understanding without fail. Illuminate my senses, let the still, small voice speak. – Ashe/Ase/Amen*

Meditation with the High Priestess – (Getting in the Receptive Mode)

Remove the High Priestess card from the Tarot deck and place the card in your hand, on your lap, or under your pillow. Reposition your body in a sitting or lying position; it is paramount to align the spine in either case. Close your eyes and take three complete, full belly breaths, by inhaling through the nose and exhaling through the mouth. Return to normal breathing as you take your fourth breath and continue this circular breathing motion while relaxing your entire body. Let sweet relaxation wash over you, starting from the top of your head and proceeding down your shoulders, arms, hands, abdomen, thighs, and legs to the soles of your feet. Feel your body breathing. Feel that unseen force enter the physical body, expanding the diaphragm, and feel the sensation of this elemental force leaving the body temple. During this time, repeat aloud or in the mind's eye the mantra, "I am open to hearing the wish of the High Priestess." Thoughts may arise; observe them and let them pass away. You may hear sounds, see visions, smell a fragrance, just allow all this to come and observe without judgment. You are now the witness, the observer. Continue to relax more deeply and let go. Immediately following the meditation, take note of any impressions, messages, images, ideas, symbols, and inspirations that you received during this exercise and list any keywords, phrases, or thoughts. Ask yourself what words describe your feelings and/or any physical sensations you experienced during the meditation; you will use these details later to capture any themes and test for convergence.

Inquire of the High Priestess – Inquire of the Lord

Now that you have done the prayer of invocation and have entered a state of meditation with the High Priestess, you are in the receptive mode. Take the High Priestess card, which will serve as the significator for this spread, and place in the appropriate position as identified in the spread chart. Take the Tarot deck and shuffle, asking, what is it that I need to *hear* concerning this situation? Once you have thoroughly shuffled the deck, cut the deck three times. Proceed to place the number of allotted cards according to the spread layout. I have provided an index to the Tarot cards' meanings in Chapter 4 to assist with interpretations. Once the cards are laid, list your initial impressions of the cards, images that stand out, and then ascertain the actual meaning of the cards from the index. Like the meditation exercise, create a list of words or phrases that describe your experiences with the cards.

Interpretation of Theme Convergence

Now that you have completed your list from your meditation and that you have completed your list based upon the Tarot spread, you will now check for convergence or correspondence. You will look for things that are showing up in both your meditation and in the actual Tarot reading – that theme developed out of the list of words or phrases, images or symbols from both the meditation and the actual reading. This theme is the message or the communication; it is the answer to the question that you are seeking to illuminate.

The goal here is to identify theme convergence and/or correspondence to corroborate the communication. Once this is done, use your intuition to determine the most reasonable and relevant messages you are receiving concerning your situation. This yields the interpretation.

The Listening spread asks, *what impedes my hearing and keeps me from being in the receptive mode?* In an example reading, the card representing this inquiry is the Two of Swords. The Two of Swords indicates the querent is closed off from something or someone; it's a very defensive posture. The aspiring healer is indecisive about moving into a more open and vulnerable space. The querent has a barrier up, and you can't get but so close to them. This is a very mental card, so this person is very much in their head and in the illusion of fear. The second question asks, *what is the message from the Higher Consciousness that I have not been hearing?* The card representing this inquiry is the Knight of Wands. The Knight of Wands gives voice to the energy of restlessness and describes the need for more focused action. This restlessness could be a result of not being obedient to your call the healing arts. The card also portends an excellent time to explore a new enterprise in the healing arts. The final question asks, *what's the lesson or insight to be gained?* The card representing this inquiry is the Eight of Pentacles. It's a message to the healer to be dedicated and committed to the perfection of their craft, and tangible success will come as a result.

Practicing this spread will help you appreciate the concept of listening and being in an open and receptive mode, in your personal and professional practice. The Tarot spread enables you to identify what you must hear clearly and adopt, as you transition into the healing arts. If you take note of the energies that came up in the Tarot spread, over time, you will see patterns emerge and be able to reconcile yourself with them. I have found the listening spread has allowed me to become an open channel and more effective in my personal and professional healing practice.

Affirmation of the High Priestess

Now that you have identified themes and have an interpretation, you are clear on the message, the insight, the lesson. The best way to actively practice and invoke this insight is to incorporate this into a daily affirmation practice. Based on the themes and the information you have received, you now can create your unique affirmation as a tribute to the High Priestess. This affirmation can be clear and simple: for example, "I am in tune and in the flow. I am open and receptive to all forms of communication, and I understand them. I know how to use the information presented to me in a positive, life-giving way."

Now that we've covered the importance of listening in an open and receptive mode, and started the work of identifying themes and solutions to clear hearing, let's dive into the importance of acceptance as you transition to your path of authority.

Chapter 8

Acceptance is Calling

Insights from Death

During my journey to self-discovery, I came across so many articles and books that expressed varying insights and perspectives. However, none were more illuminating than the concept of acceptance. I was initially exposed to this idea many years ago, during a very difficult time in my adult life. I was in the process of trying to heal and transition from this perceived difficulty. I'd ended a relationship that, when viewed in hindsight, was not a loving and supportive experience. It was painful and it was no doubt a catalyst, shifting me into having a better relationship with my higher self, resulting in a path towards alignment with my higher calling.

During this time, I was seeking direction and clarity about the journey ahead. It seemed as if I was always searching for something, and in truth, I didn't even know what it was or why. The answers to those questions had not fully taken shape. But the questions, I was certain, surrounded my very being, my very understanding of reality, and my purpose in it.

One day, I was led to a bookstore in Arlington, Virginia, to a place called *The Sacred Circle*, a magical place. I would frequent it for spiritual readings from time to time to help me get some insight on one issue or another. This one particular day, I was perusing the selection of books and suddenly, as if out of nowhere amidst this vast array of books, I discovered a book called *That Which You Are Seeking Is Seeking You!* The words in the title alone stopped me in my tracks. I wanted to cry. These would be tears of joy, hopefulness, and downright gratefulness, for I knew at that moment the healing hand of the Source that sustains all was guiding and directing, answering my call for clarity, understanding, and purpose.

The book discussed many things, but the most instrumental and life-changing were the ideas of acceptance – acceptance of what is. This lesson, for me, would go on to shape how I saw myself in this world, how I saw others, and further, how I chose to react to the things that would pop in the most unanticipated ways.

The act of acceptance is a true step towards the door of liberation. Accepting gives you freedom from all that hides you and allows you the chance to take control and chart your reality. It allows you to see things clear-eyed from a complete perspective. Accepting is a clearing exercise that allows you to see what's before you, fully.

What is Acceptance

I look at acceptance from two points of view, and both provide insight for healing and transition, for they offer a tool for course correction. The first definition is the action of consenting to receive or undertake something offered. Now, your question may be, what is the offer? What are you receiving? I would submit to you, dear one, that your very existence is the offering – those sleepless nights when the voice of longing whispers to you with a continuous gnawing. It's the undeniable thirst for manifestation calling to you; this is the voice of the master requesting you, offering you an opportunity to experience the fullness of your potential. Like in the scriptures of old, "Take up your bed and walk." You must accept yourself and all the gifts you possess and accept the call. In this, there is healing; in this, there is transformation. This metamorphosis is a result of you truly honoring your maker and the healing light that dwells within. The process of acceptance shifts the energy to bring about the opportunity to be in perfect alignment with your path.

The second definition of acceptance is the act or process of being received as adequate or suitable. You must accept the truth of who you are as God's realized being, and, I would submit, the greatest gift to humanity, for there is only one uniquely formed you. You must accept that you are enough, a perfect expression of God's infinite possibility. You are worthy, and it is demanded of you to bring about healing and transformation to the human world. In doing so, you are in perfect alignment with the Source within.

Take pride and comfort in this knowing. You are accepted by the only energy that matters and have always been, approved by the only Source that is; therefore, believe in yourself and walk in your acceptances. Acceptance of *what is,* is always the way to freedom, allowing you to come into your healing, and this, in turn, heals the world.

Acceptance is the way to salvation; it's the door to the miracle of manifestation; it's the acknowledgment of your own deeply held truth. It's a truth that your soul desires you to remember as you journey through this human land of forgetfulness. Your soul has a great deal of urgency for action – action required in both realms of existence: the realm of the spirit, and so, too, the realm of the corporal flesh. It's been said by the ancients, "As above, so below; as below, so above," – a long-held truth understood by the esoteric teacher and students of truth. Perceive this in your mind, while believing in your heart, and match it with sincere efforts by the earthen form to bring about requested reality.

Accept the Call

The first step to the healing path is to accept the call, to fully acknowledge that this path is what will soothe the soul's yearning. To know that you have a gift and not honor it is a betrayal to your Maker's hands – the Source within who shaped you. Up until now, you felt distressed, lost, afraid of the perceived bondage of the monotony of life because you did not accept. The path of the healer has been calling to you. In your acceptance, there is healing and opportunity for true transformation. This energetic transition truly honors the Creator and brings about the opportunity to be perfectly aligned with your path.

Let today be the moment you accept and let go. Let go of the fears, the lies, and the pain, let go of the resistance withholding your birthright from you. Sometimes, life presents to us a relative truth, an experience that cracks us open to the core of our very being, in the most ravaging and forceful of ways, so that we may experience the bliss of unforgettable freedom. We attain this freedom when we accept, letting go of the doubt and insecurity; then, we will have achieved the world.

This realization was the beginning of my sincere pursuit and acceptance of my healing call by walking into my purpose. I became a soul, transformed, and transmuted by all the elements above and below. I believe this concept to be full of power that will provide you strength and perspective for the journey. Take heart, forged through the fires we are, and in acceptance reborn, and with this deep knowing perfected. Accept the call, take up your bed, and answer the healing call.

A Call to Listen

I had another client, named Allen, and he wanted to invest in some land with his fiancée. He was excited about their union. He wanted to know if investing in property together was a good idea before they got married. The Tarot showed me some reluctance on the part of his partner. Allen's energy seemed to be moving full steam ahead. I tried to explain the engagement was still a bit overwhelming for his partner and that she still had some barriers up that she needs to come to terms with and reconcile her conflict. I also expressed that he was very much like Emperor energy in the relationship, meaning he was very much controlling. I advised him that he needed to slow things down. I expressed to him the likely outcome of this investment would not be favorable, and the partner was afraid because she was not fully committed to the relationship in her heart.

Some months later, I did a follow-up consultation. Allen was excited to inform me that they would no longer invest in the property together. His partner had admitted she was not ready to get married and didn't want to purchase the property together because she still had some trust and commitment issue to resolve. He expressed that he is working on not being so controlling in the relationship. It was during this time that the querent found an appreciation and respect for the guidance that the Tarot provides, and now he's included this personal development tool as a part of his daily practice.

The Transformative Energy of Acceptance

The Tarot teaches us through the Major Arcana about the transformative power of acceptance. The Tower, Death, the Hanged Man, and the World are powerful energies that, on their face, evoke change and at their root, demand acceptance. Then the full potential of their transformative power can become evident and perfectly manifested into the life of the querent.

The Tower is reminiscent of the Tower of Babel. It says to us that what mortals have built all on their own cannot stand the test of time if it's not the will of the Master Creator. The hand of God has sent fire from heaven to shake up your impermanent reality, a reality that is not in alignment with your destiny. The shock of the fiery blow has sent you hurling from the tower, set asunder, and naturally, you are in a state of shock. The message here is: Time's up. It's now time to focus on building a life in perfect harmony with the Master Weaver of creation. It's time to accept that what was is no longer; it's time to start anew.

The Death card reinforces this idea of endings and new beginnings. For you to begin on the path of alignment with Divine Order, you must let go of all that is not serving you. Let it all die so that a new life, a new perspective, and a new opportunity can be born from the ashes. The Hanged Man speaks to us of acceptance and a chosen sacrifice: you have decided to surrender to a different point of view because you know it's for the best, and this shift is preparing you for what you truly desire. You must accept the change and yield to the transformative and transitioning power of acceptance, and then you will have achieved the World.

The World is a card of completion and fulfillment; its very expression is a tribute to heaven and earth in perfect harmony.

As you read this chapter, you might have heard the clarion call from within instructing you on all that you need to accept to prepare to transition past this stagnation, this rut you feel you are existing in. Others may not have a clue, and that's okay. This process takes some honest soul communion to identify and speak the truth. I've provided a Tarot spread called, "What must I accept?" The spread will help you get clear about what it is you need to accept to facilitate your healing and transition into the healing arts.

Tarot Spread: Introduction of Death

The objective of the five-card "Acceptance" spread is to provide the querent with clarity. What is it they must accept? The Death card serves as the dedicated significator card. This Major Arcana was chosen to represent the shedding or release of something that no longer serves your interest. It's about death and birth. If you add the optional cards, they speak to changes and endings, a coming to terms, or a revelation. The Tarot spread asks the following:

1) *What is it that I know I must accept?*
2) *What are the consequences of not accepting?*
3) *How will I feel when I accept it?*
4) *What is the advice?*

Figure 2: The Acceptance Spread

Preparing to Accept

Invocation to Death

As you begin your journey to connect and attune to the energy of Death, it's essential to create space to receive her insight. The initial step is the prayer of invocation. This is the point where you call upon the God of your understanding to intervene and come to your aid. The following prayer should be done before your meditation exercise and the drawing of cards. The ritual of prayer sets an intention and invites your team to assist you as you attempt to connect deeper to the source that permeates all. Repeat the following prayer or replace it with one that resonates with you more.

> *Death is upon me and I am her friend. The old world is no longer, and the shift towards a new life is upon me. I have choices to render, and I need clarity. Grant me the courage to accept what is and what is not. Lord of Illumination, the master weaver of fate, help me to gain a clear understanding of what it is that I must accept and give me the strength to honor the request. – Ashe/Ase/Amen*

Meditation with Death (Getting in the Receptive Mode)

Remove the Death card from the Tarot deck and place the card in your hand, on your lap, or under your pillow. Reposition your body in a sitting or lying position; it is paramount to align the spine in either case. Close your eyes, take three complete, full belly breaths, by inhaling through the nose and exhaling through the mouth. Return to normal breathing as you take your fourth breath and continue this circular breathing motion while relaxing your entire body. Let sweet relaxation wash over you, starting from the top of your head and proceeding down your shoulders, arms, hands, abdomen, thighs, and legs to the soles of your feet. Feel your body breathing. Feel that unseen force enter the physical body, expanding the diaphragm and feeling the sensation of this elemental force leaving the body temple. During this time, repeat aloud or in the mind's eye the mantra, "I accept what is." Thoughts may arise. Observe them and let them pass away. You may hear sounds, see visions, smell a fragrance; allow all this to come and observe without judgment. You are now the witness, the observer. Continue to relax deeper and let go. Immediately following the meditation, take note of any impressions, messages, images, ideas, symbols, and inspirations that you received during this exercise and list any keywords, phrases, or thoughts. Ask yourself what words describe your feelings and/or any physical sensations you experienced during the meditation; you will use these details later to capture any themes and test for convergence.

Inquire of Death

Now that you have done the prayer of invocation, and have entered a state of meditation with Death, you are in the receptive mode. Take the Death card, which will serve as the significator for this spread, and place in the appropriate position as identified in the spread chart. Take the Tarot deck and shuffle, asking, "What is it that I must *accept* concerning this situation?" Once you have thoroughly shuffled the deck, cut the deck three times. Proceed to place the number of allotted cards according to the spread layout. I have provided an index to the Tarot cards' meanings in Chapter 4 to assist with interpretations. Once the cards are laid, list your initial impressions of the cards, images that stand out, and then ascertain the actual meaning of the cards from the index. Like the meditation exercise, create a list of words or phrases that describe your experiences with the cards.

Interpretation of Theme Convergence

Now that you have completed your list from your meditation and that you have completed your list based upon the Tarot spread, you will now check for convergence or correspondence. You will be looking for things that are showing up in both your meditation and in the actual Tarot reading: those themes developed out of the lists of words or phrases, images, or symbols from both the meditation and the actual reading. The theme is the message or the communication; it is the answer to the question that you are seeking to illuminate. The goal here is to identify theme convergence and/or correspondence to corroborate the communication. Once this is done, use your intuition to determine the most reasonable and relevant messages you are receiving concerning your situation. This yields the interpretation.

The Acceptance spread asks, *what is it that I know I must accept?* In an example reading, the card representing this inquiry is the Hierophant. The Hierophant indicates the querent needs to accept their destiny as a leader in society, a healer, and a teacher of a spiritual practice. The second question asks, *what are the consequences of not accepting?* The card representing this inquiry is the Nine of Swords and indicates a period of anxiety and mental stress. It suggests that if you don't follow the guidance, you will have a challenging experience filled with mental exhaustion and possibly of sleepless nights. The third card asks, *how will I feel when I accept it?* The card representing this inquiry is the Sun; it's a message to the healer of joy, happiness, and alignment, as a result of accepting. The final card asks, *what is the advice?* The card representing this inquiry is the Hanged Man. It reinforces the idea of sacrifice and the need to let go of something. It portends achieving a goal, as a result of sacrifice.

Practicing this spread will help you appreciate the concept of acceptance, and the ideas it represents for you. The spread will help you identify and acknowledge all that you must come to accept, as you transition into the healing arts. If you take note of the energies that came up in the tarot spread, over time, you will see patterns emerge and be able to reconcile yourself with them. I have found that finally accepting that I'm a gifted Tarotist lets me share my readings with more confidence and conviction.

Affirmation of Death

Now that you have identified themes and have an interpretation, you are clear on the message, the insight, the lesson. The best way to actively practice and invoke this insight is to incorporate this into a daily affirmation practice. Based on the themes and the information you have received, you can now create your unique affirmation as a tribute to Death. This affirmation can be clear and simple: for example, "I accept myself and the clarity of my calling as a Healer."

Now that we've covered the importance of accepting, and started the work identifying themes and solutions for acceptance, let's dive into the importance of grounding in compassion.

Chapter 9

Grounding in the Energy of Compassion

Insights from Strength

Compassion is the ability to exude intense feelings of concern, kindness, understanding, and mercy when navigating the human experience. The archetypical root of this expression is love. Webster defines compassion as a sympathetic consciousness of others' distress together with a desire to alleviate it. For contextualization, we call this compassionate love: a sincere affection for self and those with whom our lives are deeply intertwined. Existence is a tapestry of oneness; therefore, this compassion is directed and available to all. This concept is also about understanding that sometimes compassion takes strength and sacrifice.

To be grounded as a healer is essential for being a conduit for healing. To be grounded in the energy of compassion means moving in this life with a sincere desire to be rooted in the highest vibrational energy of love, expressed by the attitude of compassion. I submit to you that you have to believe in your heart that the Divine Intelligence / Source energy is only loving. Providing only love for you, Source will have compassion for your perceived difficulty and will support your desire to transition from the rut of stagnation into the path of your calling. Having this trust resting in your heart, you must show up in the world in-kind, with an attitude of compassion for your earthly neighbors and for yourself.

The Transitioning Power of Self -Compassion

It is a great act of self-compassion when you honor your gift and choose to remove yourself from people, places, and opportunities that don't serve you, are unfulfilling, and place you out of balance with your healing path. Self-compassion is demonstrating self-forgiveness. Forgive yourself for ignoring the still, small voice all these years, for being disobedient to the call for service. Forgive yourself for not practicing and homing in on your gift well before now. Forgive yourself for not accepting, grant yourself reprieve for not honoring the unique and authentic light of God that dwells within you. Absolve yourself for all the lies and the fears that you allowed to hold you back until now. Realize all that matters are the present moment and what you choose to do with this newfound illumination.

Self-forgiveness is a demonstration of worthiness and a conduit for transformation because we have now rid ourselves from the illusion of unworthiness. Energetically, forgiveness is unifying. It allows one to free themselves from the bonds of negative energy thoughtforms that create the perception of separation, which can cause havoc on the energy field. Forgiveness is a true gateway to liberation. Free your mind and your soul, believing in your heart, and the divine intelligence will reward your faithfulness and show in-kind compassion for your sacrifice.

Compassionate love will be required as you transition to the healing arts, and it will ground you and support your healing practice. Approaching those you serve with an attitude of compassionate love limits judgment and creates openness and receptivity – the foundational attributes of a healer. If a healer can't connect and reach the souls of another, their gift is a waste, ineffective, and not ready for the task before them.

The Tarot reflects the essence of compassion in the form of the Strength card, the eighth card in the Major Arcana. The Strength card illustrates a maiden with an infinity symbol above her head, gently taming, and closing the mouth of a lion, with calmness and ease, with her bare hands. Strength speaks to taming the beast within, and this card tells us you must channel the higher self, the higher consciousness, to respond to the world around you. It's about expressing love and, from love, mercy, forgiveness, understanding, and kindness.

Strength allows you to have better judgment, keeping you grounded in peace, offering the opportunity to bring you further into alignment with the healing heart.

My client Donny perfected this insight within me during our work together. Have you ever had to work with someone very knowledgeable and ever the opinionated one? Well, that was Donny. He had the energy of an Emperor; he was very strong in his views; he's what you would call a know-it-all. He never took responsibility for the role he played in all his unfortunate affairs. Imagine being a physician supporting the four of cups, a self -absorbed patient, a patient who feels like he knows more than the doctor. Like the Emperor, he always has his answer and he is convinced it is the right position.

When dealing with clients of this nature, compassion is the only way. Otherwise, you will end up in an ego boxing match. Your ability to express such compassion is a reflection on you and your willingness to seek healing and not ego gratification.

Ultimately, compassion is about achieving peace, harmony, and balance. By surrendering to *what is*, we lose nothing in surrender, but gain everything; for love is all there truly is. Its energy is capable of creating endless possibilities. I submit to you it is a clearing force and the ultimate transitioning power.

I've provided a Tarot spread called, "Towards what do I need to show compassion?" The spread will help you get clear about what it is you need to love and to have compassion towards to facilitate your healing and transition into the healing arts.

Tarot Spread: Introduction of Strength

The objective of the four-card Grounding spread is to provide the querent clarity on *towards what do you need to show compassion*? The Strength card serves as the dedicated significator card. This Major Arcana was chosen to represent compassion, compromises, understanding, the ability to tame the beast within, and yielding to higher consciousness. It is the embodiment of mercy and kindness. The root of Strength is love. The Tarot spread asks the following:

1. *Towards what do I need to show compassion?*
2. *What challenges my grounding?*
3. *What grounds me?*
4. *What's the insight/advice?*

Significator Card

Figure 3: The Compassion Spread

Preparing to Ground

Invocation to Strength

As you begin your journey to connect and attune to the energy of Strength, it's essential to create space to receive her insight. The initial step is the prayer of invocation. This is the point where you call upon the God of your understanding to intervene and come to your aid. The following prayer should be done before your meditation exercise and the drawing of cards. The ritual of prayer sets an intention and invites your team to assist you as you attempt to connect deeper to the Source that permeates all. Repeat the following prayer or replace it with one that resonates with you more.

> *Ground me in Strength, ground me in thee. Let my very Being be grounded eternally. Let my heart sing of the fullness of thy invigorating power, flowing abundantly through me. Let my every breath take flight, a constant conduit to the light. Let my words and deeds be forever rooted, grounded in She. – Ashe/Ase/Amen*

Meditation with Strength

Remove the Strength card from the Tarot deck and place the card in your hand, on your lap, or under your pillow. Reposition your body in a sitting or lying position; it is paramount to align the spine in either case. Close your eyes, take three complete, full belly breaths, by inhaling through the nose and exhaling through the mouth. Return to normal breathing as you take your fourth breath and continue this circular breathing motion while relaxing your entire body. Let sweet relaxation wash over you, starting from the top of your head and proceeding down your shoulders, arms, hands, abdomen, thighs, and legs to the soles of your feet. Feel your body breathing. Feel that unseen force enter the physical body, expanding the diaphragm and feeling the sensation of this elemental force leaving the body temple. During this time, repeat aloud or in the mind's eye the mantra, "I am grounded in compassion." Thoughts may arise. Observe them, and let them pass away. You may hear sounds, see visions, smell a fragrance; allow all this to come and observe without judgment. You are now the witness, the observer. Continue to relax deeper and let go. Immediately following the meditation, take note of any impressions, messages, images, ideas, symbols, and inspirations that you received during this exercise and list any keywords, phrases, or thoughts. Ask yourself what words describe your feelings and/or any physical sensations you experienced during the meditation; you will use these details later to capture any themes and test for convergence.

Inquire of Strength

Now that you have done the prayer of invocation, and have entered a state of meditation with Strength, you are in the receptive mode. Take the Strength card, which will serve as the significator for this spread and place it in the appropriate position as identified in the spread chart. Take the Tarot deck and shuffle, asking, "What is it that I must show *compassion* towards concerning this situation?" Once you have thoroughly shuffled the deck, cut the deck three times. Proceed to place the number of allotted cards according to the spread layout. I have provided an index to the Tarot cards' meanings in Chapter 4 to assist with interpretations. Once the cards are laid, list your initial impressions of the cards, and any images that stand out, and then ascertain the actual meaning of the cards from the index. Like the meditation exercise, create a list of words or phrases that describe your experiences with the cards.

Interpretation of Theme Convergence

Now that you have completed your list from your meditation and that you have completed your list based upon the Tarot spread, you will now check for convergence or correspondence. You will be looking for things that are showing up in both your meditation and in the actual Tarot reading: those themes developed out of list of words or phrases, images, or symbols from both the meditation and the actual reading. The theme is the message or the communication; it is the answer to the question that you are seeking to illuminate. The goal here is to identify theme convergence and/or correspondence to corroborate the communication. Once this is done, use your intuition to determine the most reasonable and relevant messages you are receiving concerning your situation. This yields the interpretation.

The Grounding spread asks, *towards what do I need to show compassion?* In an example reading, the card representing this inquiry is the Hermit. The Hermit indicates the querent's need for introspection and self-reflection; this card is demanding an act of love and a demonstration of self-compassion as a result of inner work. The second question asks, *What challenges my grounding?* The card representing this inquiry is the Devil. The Devil indicates a period of control and unhealthy codependency. It suggests that if you don't heed the guidance and remove yourself from unhealthy and controlling experiences (i.e. toxic work and personal relationships), the Devil will compromise your grounding. The third card asks, *what grounds me?* The card representing this inquiry is the High Priestess; it's a message to the healer of meditation and getting into a practice of stillness. It's also about being grounded by working in the fields related to the esoteric. The final card asks, *What's the insight/advice?* The card representing this inquiry is the Magician. The Magician enforces your power and ability to create the conditions for your grounding and success. It indicates the manifesting power of your belief.

Practicing this spread will help you understand the level of compassion needed in your healing work. If you take note of the energies that came up in the Tarot spread, over time, you will see patterns emerge and be able to reconcile yourself with them. I have found that practicing compassion lets me share my gifts more often and effortlessly.

Affirmation of Strength

Now that you have identified themes and have an interpretation, you are clear on the message, the insight, the lesson. The best way to actively practice and invoke this insight is to incorporate this into a daily affirmation practice. Based on the themes and the information you have received, you can now create your unique affirmation as a tribute to Strength. This affirmation can be clear and simple: for example, "I am always grounded in compassion. Love always grounds me."

Now that we've covered the importance of grounding in compassion and started the work identifying themes and solutions to grounding, let's dive into the importance of self-expression.

Chapter 10

Embody the Authority
of Self-Expression

Insights from the Emperor

The law is true: we attract our "vibrational frequency." So today, perceive yourself into a different frequency. Choose to focus on being an alternate expression of Source's infinite possibility. Choose to be the healer you have longed to express. James Allen, in his work *As a Man Thinketh,* said, "Men do not attract that which they want, but that which they are." People do not attract solely based on wanting in this life experience; rather, they attract who and what they feel they are in the experience. The universe responds to this as energy with a vibrational match and attracting more of the song you sing. Ask yourself, "Who *am* I? What about me is attracting these *mirrors* as part of my life experience? Furthermore, what shall I learn from this understanding?"

We must be completely honest, even unto the pain. Gaze deliberately, yet humbly into the mirrors that are before you, then you will see and hear true self, as the miracle of awakening unfolds.

The Access Codes to Your Power

The Divine mind is a conscious system, so to speak, that responds to the codes you input, resulting in an output. This concept is consistent with systems theory. I believe having the right combination of inputs creates the opportunity to access universal power. This universal power is creative. It's intelligent and responds to the frequency that you are emanating.

I like to look at it from the lens of a video gamer. Let's take the example of a Play Station 4 (PS4) game system. I like the game Mortal Combat. In the game, there are various fighters, all having their own unique sets of abilities and powers. My favorite character is the god Raiden, by the way. His powers are accessed by keying in the right combination of inputs in perfect order.

In the same way, we have access to an untapped potential with the correct code sequence to unleash our gifts into the world and increase our chances of winning the game of life. Some gamers are playing the game with no awareness, pushing random buttons, and only by chance accessing power. Others have limited awareness but still don't fully have clear understanding of the input codes and push random buttons in the hope of assessing the power that will give them victory but they have no clue on the process that allowed them to win round one of the games.

Lastly, you have those consistent winners who understand the rules and the accurate codes to input. With that knowledge, they deliberately, and with a deep trust and confidence, activate their powers and consciously create energy capable of maintaining consistent wins; this is the mindset of the Magician.

The Magician knows the rules of the game, and he knows how to access the elements and manifest his will into the material world.

Those who wander aimlessly into the night, pushing buttons with no idea of their function or the order of operations, wonder why they are not winning at the game of life. Perhaps the reason is they don't know the rules; they don't know the codes to input to gain access. I would venture to say that access is closer than the breath and easier than we think. You are unwittingly triggering your potential, but not consistently; it's short-lived and not sustained. You have not ingested the playbook, and you are inputting random codes in the dark of night without the benefit of the light.

Now you may be asking what the codes to accessing your potential power are. Specifically, how can you access your healing power and facilitate the healing of humanity? I would submit to you that among other insights, having a belief in your authority and honoring your unique self-expression are key codes, which means having courage and faith in yourself in the face of self-doubt by honoring your true self. We are drawn from eternity into the body temple and wrapped in the authority of the light within, guided by compassionate love with self-expression serving as the active motivation and the most substantial evidence of universal gratitude.

Embracing Your Authority

Authority (The Light of God within) is defined as the emanating light of God within, expressing outward to the world as a *complete* power, affecting what it *wills*. Webster defines authority as the power to influence or command thought, opinion, or behavior. We are conceived by and in the *all* power (the absolute authority). We come into the physical world with the power to influence our internal and external happenings. We are endowed with the light of the *all*, expressed in the uniqueness of the relative self. Our authority is bound in free will. We have the option of choice, synonymous in every execution.

The Tarot provides us the essence of this authority in the form of the Emperor, the fourth card of the Major Arcana, with its energy associated with authority, power, structure, stability, security, and self-discipline. This energy possesses a great deal of confidence in his power and abilities; he is the wise and knowledgeable father, ruler of his domain. He knows best; he is the expert in his field, and he is confident about who he is and what he has to contribute to the world. He sits on his throne with clarity, an assuredness about his rule.

So, you must come into alignment with the Emperor within. You must understand and own your self-worth and know the value you have come into this world to share with humanity. You must own your gifts and express them without fear and insecurity. You must command them by your will. Having this awareness, the healer within with all their gifts and talents can slumber no more in the face of fear and discontent, having come into the presence of their power.

I became the Emperor a few years ago, when I decide to start my part-time professional healing practice as a Tarotist and Reiki practitioner. I proclaimed to the world that I am an authority in the Tarot. Every client reading I participated in, I leaned in with power. I become ever more confident in my abilities after each session. Soon, after launching my Tarot business, I began to travel and participate in various festivals and expos across the country. As a result of honoring my soul's calling, it didn't take long for me to develop such a good reputation in the field, and I was invited on my first international business trip to the island of Curacao, to perform Tarot readings for the public. When you walk in the Emperor's authority, the universe will conspire to reinforce your power by stretching the bounds of your domain.

The Power of Unique Self-Expression (The Relative Authentic Self)

Webster defines self-expression as the expression of one's personality. Self-Expression is the active representation of the *complete* identified self, embodying experiences, thoughts, feelings, and behaviors, manifesting in a uniquely formed individual expression. Self-expression serves as the active motivation in the human experience and as the strongest evidence of universal gratitude. Self-expression is about showing up as you are without fear or judgment; it's about expressing in all your ways from a space of courage and liberation. It's about knowing that just as I am, I am complete and beautiful in my unique way. It's about marching to the beat of your drum. In this case, it is about moving towards your healing call, with courage, undergirded with a strong faith and confidence in the self. The Tarot reminds us of the importance of owning and being confident about who you are. It's about standing your ground in the fullness of who you are.

The Fool card, number zero of the Major Arcana, is the greatest example of self- expression. He walks effortlessly and easily on his way, liberated from the bonds of fear and anticipation. He is joyous and excited about the adventure ahead. He leaps from the cliff without a care in the world. He exists fully without reservation within his authentic self.

The more you walk in the authentic light of divine consciousness without fear, the more the idea of heaven being here and now will become real to you. Awakening allows us to come into the *truth* that we are the master weavers of this tapestry of experience we call life. The manipulation and mastery of our life experiences begin at the point of realizing that *all* is energy; as such, all encounters and observations should be viewed from this proper perspective.

Whether we are aware of this fundamental framework of the Law or not, the authentic expression of our divine self has an energy associated with it, and with that awakening and realization comes great opportunity to create true change in this human experience we have chosen. For me, this is the critical reason behind my almost innate need and desperate desire to remember who I truly am and from whence I came. We are more than flesh and bones, far more. The greatest of all accomplishments that we could ever attain in this level of existence is the realization of this powerful, transformative, elusive truth. We believe in so many things perceived to be external to our opportunity of life – why not truly believe in *yourself*? Is it so hard to *believe* and *know* the true power that dwells within? This true power is affecting all life experiences, and you are your greatest impediment to the realization of this true power here and now. Only illusion stands between you and all the love, peace, joy, and true abundance that you in *truth* already are and have always been. Can't you feel it?

This realization can easily begin with the observation of

your divine breath. Just Believe, Know, Feel, and Be fully the light that you are.

I've provided a Tarot spread called, "How can I embody my Authority?" It will help you get clear about how you need to be expressing in this world to facilitate your healing and prepare to transition into the healing arts.

Tarot Spread: Introduction of the Emperor

The objective of the seven-card Authority spread is to provide the querent the opportunity to gain clarity on *how to embody your authority*? The Emperor card serves as the dedicated significator card. This Major Arcana was chosen to represent authority, order, rulership, worldly power, and the ability to master and control your domain. It's the energy of the confident, wise, knowledgeable father. The Tarot spread asks the following:

1. *What is my authority?*
2. *What challenges my authority?*
3. *What enhances my authority?*
4. *What will align me with my authority?*
5. *What is the insight/lesson?*
6. *What is the outcome?*

Figure 4: The Authority Spread

Preparing to Ground

Invocation to the Emperor

As you begin your journey to connect and attune to the energy of the Emperor, it's essential to create space to receive his insight. The initial step is the prayer of invocation. This is the point where you call upon the God of your understanding to intervene and come to your aid. The following prayer should be done before your meditation exercise and the drawing of cards. The ritual of prayer sets an intention and invites your team to assist you as you attempt to connect deeper to the Source that permeates all. Repeat the following prayer or replace it with one that resonates with you more.

> *Father I call to thee, oh firmly fixed protector, guardian of the realm of me, I call to the Emperor. Let your wisdom and authority wash over me; let your authority ground me in thee. Let my very Being reflect the authority that is my self-expression. – Ashe/Ase/ Amen*

Meditation with Authority

Remove the Emperor card from the Tarot deck and place the card in your hand, on your lap, or under your pillow. Reposition your body in a sitting or lying position; it is paramount to align the spine in either case. Close your eyes, take three complete, full belly breaths, by inhaling through the nose and exhaling through the mouth. Return to normal breathing as you take your fourth breath and continue this circular breathing motion while relaxing your entire body. Let sweet relaxation wash over you, starting from the top of your head and proceeding down your shoulders, arms, hands, abdomen, thighs, and legs to the soles of your feet. Feel your body breathing. Feel that unseen force enter the physical body, expanding the diaphragm and feeling the sensation of this elemental force leaving the body temple. During this time, repeat aloud or in the mind's eye the mantra, "I embody the authority of self-expression." Thoughts may arise. Observe them and let them pass away. You may hear sounds, see visions, smell a fragrance; allow all this to come and observe without judgment. You are now the witness, the observer. Continue to relax deeper and let go. Immediately following the meditation, take note of any impressions, messages, images, ideas, symbols, and inspirations that you received during this exercise and list any keywords, phrases, or thoughts. Ask yourself what words describe your feelings and/or any physical sensations you experienced during the meditation; you will use these details later to capture any themes and test for convergence.

Inquire of the Emperor

Now that you have done the prayer of invocation and have entered a state of meditation with the Emperor, you are in the receptive mode. Take the Emperor card, which will serve as the significator for this spread, and place it in the appropriate position as identified in the spread chart. Take the Tarot deck and shuffle, asking, "What is it that I must embody in this situation?" Once you have thoroughly shuffled the deck, cut the deck three times. Proceed to place the number of allotted cards according to the spread layout. I have provided an index to the Tarot cards' meanings in Chapter 4 to assist with interpretations. Once the cards are laid, list your initial impressions of the cards, and any images that stand out, and then ascertain the actual meaning of the cards from the index. Like the meditation exercise, create a list of words or phrases that describe your experiences with the cards.

Interpretation of Theme Convergence

Now that you have completed your list from your meditation and that you have completed your list based upon the Tarot spread, you will now check for convergence or correspondence. You will be looking for things that are showing up in both your meditation and in the actual Tarot reading: those themes developed out of the lists of words or phrases, images, or symbols from both the meditation and the actual reading. The theme is the message or the communication; it is the answer to the question that you are seeking to illuminate. The goal here is to identify theme convergence and/or correspondence to corroborate the communication. Once this is done, use your intuition to determine the most reasonable and relevant messages you are receiving concerning your situation. This yields the interpretation.

The Authority spread asks, *what is my authority?* In an example reading, the card representing this inquiry is the Queen of Swords. The Queen of Swords indicates the querent's need to channel the energy of clear and wise communication; your authority is within your speech and your life experiences. The querent can command the attention of all who hear your expressions. Your power reflects in your ability to be firm, fair, and always honest. The second question asks, *What challenges*

107

my authority? The card representing this inquiry is the Seven of Cups. The Seven of Cups indicates a period of lack of focus and wishful thinking about a project; the project could be starting a part-time healing practice, allowing you to facilitate healing through your expressed communications. This card suggests that a lack of focus could challenge this project and cause project failure because you didn't have the necessary single-mindedness. The third card asks, *What enhances my authority?* The card representing this inquiry is the Star; it's a message to the healer of faith and divine spiritual connection. It's also about understanding that Source energy will renew and rejuvenate your being and enhance your gifts if you seek after your team. The message is we hear your prayer, and we are here to assist. The fourth card asks, *what will align me with my authority?* The card representing this inquiry is the Seven of Wands. The Seven of Wands is telling the querent to stand up for your passions, defend your position, by being active and courageous. It means defending your creative energy and peace of mind from negative and hostile opposition. The fifth card asks, *what is the insight/lesson?* Represented by the Four of Pentacles, the message is to take control of your finances by being prudent and practical. It's about feeling safe and secure in the real world. This card could be telling the aspiring healer to be strategic and wise with transition plans. The final card asks, *what is the outcome?* The card representing this inquiry is the Six of Wands. The Six of Wands speaks to leadership and triumph. The querent has achieved victory and progress after taking a risk.

Practicing this spread will help you learn to embody the energies required in your healing work. If you take note of the energies that came up in the Tarot spread, over time, you will see patterns emerge and be able to reconcile yourself with them. I have found embodying my authority lets me share my gifts more often and more powerfully.

Affirmation of the Emperor

Now that you have identified themes and have an interpretation, you are clear on the message, the insight, the lesson. The best way to actively practice and invoke this insight is to incorporate this into a daily affirmation practice. Based on the themes and the information you have received, you can now create your unique affirmation as a tribute to Strength. This affirmation can be clear and simple: for example, "I embody the authority of my own self-expression" or "I am in control of my domain."

Now that we've covered the authority of your self-expression, let's dive into the power of your will.

Chapter 11

Focusing the Will

Insights from the Chariot

$\mathcal{F}$ocus the light. Indeed, you are the light. Identify your target and aim true. Be the archer and let your thoughts, your wishes, and your sincere desire be the arrow. Let your emotions be the bow and, in perfect alignment, reach the targeted goal. You are the light in the darkness; your very essence brings a field of illumination. You need only look, commanding the light within, shining forth from eternity. Eternity, how beautiful it is, as the stars sparkle in the night sky, gleaming through the void of space; so too we shimmer in their midst. In the darkness dwells potential, a silent stirring, waiting to birth the radiant possibility of the eternal flame. What is this flame that burns without end? It is an endless, ever-present power that imbues creation. It is the source of intricacy and effortless being. Command and wait with patience, to see eternity unveiled. It is the unveiling that removes shadows, bringing forth illumination of the soul. The soul shines like the sun casting away the darkness.

Believe on this and existence shall be like the womb of the Mother, expanding with constant nurturing. When you focus the light, you bring attention to a subject, and the universe will respond to this call. You want fulfillment in your personal and professional life, and you seek to explore your healing gifts.

You seek to touch the lives of humanity by starting your healing practice; therefore focus the light. It is only by a deliberate focus that the universe will respond and conspire to make all things desired and actively sought after manifested. Energy goes where your attention flows. What you think about, you bring about.

I'm sure you have witnessed the power of human manifestation in everyday life, for example, when you think about not wanting bills and lack, what do you get? More expenses and more demands compounded by unexpected bills and more lack. Why? Because you keep telling the story of how hard it is, how overwhelmed you feel, how all you ever get in the mail is bills. Well, the Universal Consciousness says, as you command. Perhaps your job is stressful, and all you talk about is how stressful and demanding your situation is, well, ever wonder, why your boss is poking at you driving you to the brink of insanity? You keep asking them to. Universal Consciousness is responding to your request of "what I don't want" with yes, you do, here you go.

Manifestation can work the other way around where you manifest something positive and actually in line with what you want. I wanted a doctorate by the time I was 30 years old. I wanted to be a homeowner before my 30th birthday. I want to establish a viable part time business before I was 30 years of age. I wanted to write a book before 35 years old, and I wanted to have a closer relationship with my little brother ASAP. I manifested that list, and more, and all it took was a thoughtform and sincere belief to cause the Universal Consciousness to respond and conspire in my favor. I reacted to every situation and opportunity of favor coming to me.

Every action would propel me closer and closer to bring my goals to fruition.

It is your natural power, your birthright as a creation: a thoughtform perceived and manifested in and from the mind of God. So, too, you are a creator, and all you perceive has the potential of being manifested in this human experience. Indeed, you are responsible for everything you attract in this life.

Knowing this truth, you owe it to yourself to be focused and deliberative, thoughtful, and resolute in your wanting. At this moment, you must be mindful of right-minded thinking. Focus your light on the healing path and be guided by right-minded thinking, for you are a radiant light from the infinite *all*.

The problem is we let the failures and inadequacies of our humanness overshadow the only Truth that is relevant in this journey. We are the co-creators of our reality. The truth is the radiant light of the purest and most consequential reality of Love, which abides within us, for it is that Truth abiding within, which is effortless and unconditionally eternal. Love is always granting the opportunity to observe all experiences without judgment and its application to limiting conditions transitions us to our true belief.

The projected will focuses the light. It's very much liked the scriptures suggest in the Old Testament when the God of Israel said, "I am that I am." This can also be read, "I will what I will be." The fact is the light changes form and takes shape according to the perceiver and transforms according to the will. The Tarot provides us the essence of this will in the form of the Chariot, the seventh card of the Major Arcana, whose energy is associated with control, willpower, success, action, and determination. The Chariot represents a coming of age; he is clear-minded, has emotional control, and is focused on his target, focused on success, and victory is within his sight. So, too, you must be. When it comes to embarking on this personal and professional journey to the healing arts, you must be the Chariot without fear and filled with focused determination and committed to the path, allowing the universe to respond to your request for movement.

I've provided a Tarot spread called, "What's my focus?" The spread will help you get clear about what it is you need to focus on to facilitate your healing and prepare for transition into the healing arts.

Tarot Spread: Introduction of the Chariot

The objective of the five-card Focus spread is to provide the querent the opportunity to gain clarity on what their focus should be at this time. The Chariot card serves as the dedicated significator card. This Major Arcana was chosen to represent balance, emotional control, willpower, and victory. It is the embodiment of mastery and focus.

1. *What is my focus at present?*
2. *Where should I focus going forward?*
3. *What will compromise my focus?*
4. *What is the insight/lesson?*

Figure 5: The Focus Spread

Preparing to Ground

Invocation of the Chariot

As you begin your journey to connect and attune to the energy of the Chariot, it's essential to create space to receive his insight. The initial step is the prayer of invocation. This is the point where you call upon the God of your understanding to intervene and come to your aid. The following prayer should be done before your meditation exercise and the drawing of cards. The ritual of prayer sets an intention and invites your team to assist you as you attempt to connect deeper to the Source that permeates all. Repeat the following prayer or replace it with one that resonates with you more.

> *Align me with the Chariot. Let the Chariot charge towards wisdom and sweet victory. Reveal to me what my focus should be at this time. Direct me towards true aims. – Ashe/Ase/Amen*

Meditation with the Chariot

Remove the Chariot card from the Tarot deck and place the card in your hand, on your lap, or under your pillow. Reposition your body in a sitting or lying position; it is paramount to align the spine in either case. Close your eyes, take three complete, full belly breaths, by inhaling through the nose and exhaling through the mouth. Return to normal breathing as you take your fourth breath and continue this circular breathing motion while relaxing your entire body. Let sweet relaxation wash over you, starting from the top of your head and proceeding down your shoulders, arms, hands, abdomen, thighs, and legs to the soles of your feet. Feel your body breathing. Feel that unseen force enter the physical body, expanding the diaphragm and feeling the sensation of this elemental force leaving the body temple. During this time, repeat aloud or in the mind's eye the mantra, "I am charging forward towards victory." Thoughts may arise. Observe them, and let them pass away. You may hear sounds, see visions, smell a fragrance; allow all this to come and observe without judgment. You are now the witness, the observer. Continue to relax deeper and let go. Immediately following the meditation, take note of any impressions, messages, images, ideas, symbols, and inspirations that you received during this exercise and list any keywords, phrases, or thoughts. Ask yourself what words describe your feelings and/or any physical sensations you experienced during the meditation; you will use these details later to capture any themes and test for convergence.

Inquire of the Chariot

Now that you have done the prayer of invocation, and have entered a state of meditation with the Chariot, you are in the receptive mode. Take the Chariot card, which will serve as the significator for this spread, and place in the appropriate position as identified in the spread chart. Take the Tarot deck and shuffle, asking, "What is it that I must focus on in this situation?" Once you have thoroughly shuffled the deck, cut the deck three times. Proceed to place the number of allotted cards according to the spread layout. I have provided an index to the Tarot cards' meanings in Chapter 4 to assist with interpretations. Once the cards are laid, list your initial impressions of the cards, and any images that stand out, and then ascertain the actual meaning of the cards from the index. Like the meditation exercise, create a list of words or phrases that describe your experiences with the cards.

Interpretation of Theme Convergence

Now that you have completed your list from your meditation and that you have completed your list based upon the Tarot spread, you will now check for convergence or correspondence. You will be looking for things that are showing up in both your meditation and in the actual Tarot reading: those themes developed out of the lists of words or phrases, images, or symbols from both the meditation and the actual reading. The theme is the message or the communication; it is the answer to the question that you are seeking to illuminate. The goal here is to identify theme convergence and/or correspondence to corroborate the communication. Once this is done, use your intuition to determine the most reasonable and relevant messages you are receiving concerning your situation. This yields the interpretation.

The Focus spread asks, *what is my focus at present?* In an example reading, the card representing this inquiry is the Two of Cups. The Two of Cup indicates the querent's focus on a harmonious partnership; this could be the healing and reconciliation of a connection. The second question asks, *where should I focus going forward?* The card representing this inquiry is Three of Wands. The Three of Wands indicates a period of planned expansion as a result of following your passion; this is the querent doing the planning for the future, possibly a collaboration with the Two of Cups figure. The third card asks, *what will compromise my focus?* The card representing this inquiry is the Five of Wands. The Five of Wands represent conflicts and instability; if this partnership is not on the same page, the tension could compromise and impede the querent's focus, as a result of not working together towards the same goals. The final card asks, *what is the insight/lesson?* The lesson represented by the Justice card. This energy speaks to the aspiring healer who needs to be fair and balanced when addressing competing interests. The message here is alignment gained as a result of truth and justice. It portends a win in your favor.

Practicing this spread will help you understand what energies you need to focus on in the course of your healing work. If you take note of the concepts that came up in the Tarot spread, over time you will see patterns emerge in what distracts you from your focus and grow ever stronger in staying on focus.

Affirmation of the Chariot

Now that you have identified themes and have an interpretation, you are clear on the message, the insight, the lesson. The best way to actively practice and invoke this insight is to incorporate this into a daily affirmation practice. Based on the themes and the information you have received, you can now create your unique affirmation as a tribute to the Chariot. This affirmation can be clear and simple: for example, "I am focused on my success."

Now that we've covered the power of a focused will, let's dive into the power of trust.

Chapter 12

Trust

Insights from the Star

In this life, if you are wise, you know to trust the words of God that dwell within you. There is a deep knowing that in all your measures, you must seek the heart of your Divine Creator for direction and strength to endure the task before you. You recognize a will far more expansive than the cognitive mind alone, so you pull from eternity towards God. I call this the Dear-God moment. We all have Dear-God moments. I have had countless, and this power saw me through them all.

I recall one, in particular, during my dissertation process; this was a time of great pressure, as achieving a doctorate was one of my most desired goals. I recall praying, "Dear God, help me out of this situation successfully." I must admit that I was tired of this dissertation process and all the twists and turns. Still, I had faith in my successful completion. I could see it in my mind's eye. No matter the difficulty, the *all* power brought me through, because I trusted in myself and the universal consciousness to respond to my request.

I submit to you, dear one, that the nature of trust is faith. You must, in all your doing, exercise a fervent faith; said another way, you must have a sincere belief in the power that you have called forth from eternity to aid in your efforts of manifestation. There exists no effective power when void of belief. You must with all your will believe in your heart all that you want will come to pass and then, as if magic – for indeed, it is the greatest of magic – the universe will move in your favor.

The scriptures tell us, "Now, faith is the substance of things hoped for, the evidence of things not seen." Therein lies an access code of creation. Faith here is the belief, a fervent trust that what you are hoping for will come to pass. What you have imagined is already on the way into existence. Now the key is to hold this dream in your heart. The longing matched with an attitude of gratitude and anticipation gives momentum to physical manifestation. It is not always necessary to understand how this works – but it is necessary to know that it *will* work – to make all your desires possible.

The challenge you have is your doubt, and when that doubt lingers for a while, you cancel the request. You have up until now lacked faith in the power that you have called forth to aid you. Indeed, you doubt yourself and your power to manifest as a co-creator. You do not believe you are worthy; you do not believe in your true potential, and the universe responds by attracting to you the very measure of what you believe.

If you believe that you are a healer and called for service, serve. If you believe that your path of service will bring you into alignment, balance, abundance, security, fulfillment, satisfaction, and peace, this it shall. You can be an instrument of peace, healing, and illumination. You can have all that you imagine and faithfully tend. So, let the words of the Christ, the way-shower, be a compass and a guiding light that will undergird your faith and sincere trust in the Spirit and the universal law that attracts to you all that you shall perceive. "No one who puts a hand to the plow and looks back is fit for service in the kingdom of God" – Luke 9:62 NIV. Looking back is evidence of doubt, fear, and a betrayal of God's power within.

I've provided a Tarot spread called, "What should I trust?" The spread will help you get clear about what it is you need to trust to facilitate your healing and prepare for transition into the healing arts.

Tarot Spread: Introduction of the Star

The objective of the six-card Trust spread is to provide the querent the opportunity to gain clarity on *what is it you should trust*? The Star card serves as the dedicated significator card. This Major Arcana was chosen to represent replenishment, higher forces, destiny, and looking ahead in faith. It is the embodiment of having faith and believing in a hopeful and positive future. The Tarot spread asks the following:

1. *What do I trust that at present is not serving me?*
2. *Where should I place my trust?*
3. *What compromises/challenges my trust?*
4. *What is the insight?*
5. *What's the outcome?*

Significator Card

Figure 6: The Trust Spread

Preparing to Ground

Invocation to the Star

As you begin your journey to connect and attune to the energy of the Star, it's essential to create space to receive her insight. The initial step is the prayer of invocation. This is the point where you call upon the God of your understanding to intervene and come to your aid. The following prayer should be done before your meditation exercise and the drawing of cards. The ritual of prayer sets an intention and invites your team to assist you as you attempt to connect deeper to the Source that permeates all. Repeat the following prayer or replace it with one that resonates with you more.

> *I call upon the Star. I invoke your awe-inspiring and restoring power. Fill me with steadfast hopefulness. Imbue me with abiding faith for a hopeful future. Reveal to me where I want faith. Increase my faith to always, let my trust be forever assured. – Ashe/Ase/ Amen*

Meditation with the Star

Remove the Star card from the Tarot deck and place the card in your hand, on your lap, or under your pillow. Reposition your body in a sitting or lying position; it is paramount to align the spine in either case. Close your eyes, take three complete, full belly breaths, by inhaling through the nose and exhaling through the mouth. Return to normal breathing as you take your fourth breath and continue this circular breathing motion while relaxing your entire body. Let sweet relaxation wash over you, starting from the top of your head and proceeding down your shoulders, arms, hands, abdomen, thighs, and legs to the soles of your feet. Feel your body breathing. Feel that unseen force enter the physical body, expanding the diaphragm and feeling the sensation of this elemental force leaving the body temple. During this time, repeat aloud or in the mind's eye the mantra, "Everything is unfolding in a positive way." Thoughts may arise. Observe them, and let them pass away. You may hear sounds, see visions, smell a fragrance; allow all this to come and observe without judgment. You are now the witness, the observer. Continue to relax deeper and let go. Immediately following the meditation, take note of any impressions, messages, images, ideas, symbols, and inspirations that you received during this exercise and list any keywords, phrases, or thoughts. Ask yourself what words describe your feelings and/or any physical sensations you experienced during the meditation; you will use these details later to capture any themes and test for convergence.

Inquire of the Star

Now that you have done the prayer of invocation, and have entered a state of meditation with the Star, you are in the receptive mode. Take the Star card, which will serve as the significator for this spread, and place it in the appropriate position as identified in the spread chart. Take the Tarot deck and shuffle, asking, "What is that I should trust in concerning this situation?" Once you have thoroughly shuffled the deck, cut the deck three times. Proceed to place the number of allotted cards according to the spread layout. I have provided an index to the Tarot cards' meanings in Chapter 4 to assist with interpretations. Once the cards are laid, list your initial impressions of the cards, and any images that stand out, and then ascertain the actual meaning of the cards from the index. Like the meditation exercise, create a list of words or phrases that describe your experiences with the card.

Interpretation of Theme Convergence

Now that you have completed your list from your meditation and that you have completed your list based upon the Tarot spread, you will now check for convergence or correspondence. You will be looking for things that are showing up in both your meditation and in the actual Tarot reading: those themes developed out of the lists of words or phrases, images, or symbols from both the meditation and the actual reading. The theme is the message or the communication; it is the answer to the question that you are seeking to illuminate. The goal here is to identify theme convergence and/or correspondence to corroborate the communication. Once this is done, use your intuition to determine the most reasonable and relevant messages you are receiving concerning your situation. This yields the interpretation.

The Trust spread asks, *what do I trust that at present is not serving me?* In an example reading, the card representing this inquiry is the Ten of Wands. Ten of Wands means you are taking on too much, and have too much pride to ask for support. It indicates that you need to learn to trust others to help actualize your goals. Your ability to reach your goals without help is compromised. The second question asks, *Where should I place my trust?* The card representing this inquiry is the Empress. The

Empress suggests that you should trust in your nurturing and emotional personality. The message here is to trust the creative and abundant ideas of the Empress. The third card asks, *What compromises/challenges my trust?*

The card representing this inquiry is the Three of Swords; it's a message to the healer to be mindful of mental distress and heartbreak; this energy speaks of anguish. The card warns the healer that this energy will compromise their goal of trusting. The Fourth card asks, *what is the insight?* The card representing this inquiry is Judgment. Judgment indicates redemption and forgiveness. The querent knows better now, and it's clear to you what makes you happy. You are living a life without regret. The final question is, *what's the outcome?* The Six of Swords indicates a need to take action to bring something to a resolution. The querent has decided to move away from what's troubling them. The aspiring healer is in transit to a place of harmony and balance.

Practicing this spread will help you understand what energies you need to trust to become active in your healing work. If you take note of the concepts that came up in the Tarot spread, over time you will see patterns emerge and be able to reconcile yourself with them. Studying this spread has allowed me to share my gifts, undergirded by faith and abiding trust in God.

Affirmation of the Star

Now that you have identified themes and have an interpretation, you are clear on the message, the insight, the lesson. The best way to actively practice and invoke this insight is to incorporate this into a daily affirmation practice. Based on the themes and the information you have received, you can now create your unique affirmation as a tribute to Judgment. This affirmation can be clear and simple: for example, "I always trust in the God in me, as me."

Now that we've covered the importance of trusting and started the work of identifying themes and solutions to ground your faith, let's dive into the importance of releasing and letting go of fear.

Chapter 13

Release and Let That Shit Go

Insights from the Fool

The Status Quo

We exist in a place and time where the status quo feels as though it must not be disturbed, and the mere mention or inquiry into why, what, where is clouded with hollow and ever-elusive concepts of advancement and upward mobility. The fact remains that the premise and the only options considered are faulty. They are perpetuating fear, disunity, disharmony, ignorance, poverty, and lack. As a consequence, the status quo prevents perfect balance and harmony with nature.

We, as people, seem to be in a constant pursuit to reach security through upward mobility by all the means available to us. There is little consideration about if that pursuit is in alignment with our mission in this world. Our purpose for being is the foundational and defining factor of our fulfillment in the human experience, and we are no doubt oblivious to how truly disadvantaged and exploited we are as we slumber. It feels as though the system we live in seeks to undermine the internal hopes and aspirations of a people. We are like mindless cogs in a wheel, seeking salvation from the monotony of life's demands.

I have come to suspect the system is designed to keep us asleep. It seeks to deny us the freedom that comes from the servant heart, and this denial is birthed out of the perpetuation of fear of the conscious soul. But the spirit within continues to call you, it continues to invite a deep yearning for more. This yearning that causes one to experience distress and sadness is a consequence for behaving out of balance: you are not in alignment with Divine Harmony.

The perpetuation of greed, fear, and lack of respect for the human spirit has become so prevalent that the people cannot imagine life as we know to be any different; this leads to a state of hopelessness. It's systemic, to the point that cogitating on ideas of dynamic change, leading to the good of all humanity and the destruction of so many constructs, is a radical point of view. Truth, Love, Fairness, Honesty, Compassion, and Oneness have become radical ideas. If indeed this moment is upon us and we yield to the fear, and we concede that there is no other course before us, we have doomed humanity to an unawakenable sleep where the egoic mind has dominance. We now view our unfulfilled daily realities as the price of existence in the matrix of life.

But there are those light-bearers – healers like those of you reading this text – who are desperately seeking to awaken, no longer willing to exist out of alignment with their healing purpose. We healers have accepted our calling to speak our truth until we have served our purpose in this human form. So, yield not to the insecurity of fear, be focused in your just cause, and without fear in your heart, present your entire being, and know that the divine order will sustain your surrender to your path. Go in peace and bestow your healing light unto all life, be the light unto the darkness. Fear and insecurity have no place. Be ruled by divine intelligence.

It has become natural to the human experience that as we begin to take action towards accepting and expressing our God-realized potential, we begin to experience feelings of fear and uncertainty. You will doubt yourself, but hope prevails if you trust, and the fear subsides. It is my fervent hope that today, you will begin to feel a stillness taking root inside and that this stillness will take you far away from the world that no longer serves your highest good. I pray that this stillness will give you the freedom of existence – the existence you have been longing for. You lack nothing; you are moving towards the remembrance of your perfect form, the perfection that you already are, a perfection that is the alignment of your path. The Creator has left you a gift: the freedom to choose. There seem to be many options before you, but there is only, truly one path to fulfillment, and once aligned, you will find that all the worries, the fear, and the negative chatter have been washed away by God's healing waters.

Let the healer rise from within and be complete in this life. The work will be gratifying in your sight, and peace will be given for your sacrifice of trust.

The Material World of Fear

The Pentacles in the Tarot represent the material world; when they show up in a spread, they are the evidence of our manifesting power in the material world. The only thing that will impede your preparation work and your successful transition towards the healing path is fear. Fear is the number one killer of dreams. Our fears keep us wrapped in a cocoon of impossibility. You are God's infinite possibility in the body, but what is infinite possibility unwilled and unfocused? It's a waste of potential. Insecurity about your gift is a real fear; self-worth is a real challenge.

Some people fear the Tarot or any form of divination; in other words, they don't want to know; they don't want to listen to the still, small voice of the subconscious mind. This causes them to be afraid; they are concerned about what may be revealed to them. Said another way, you are afraid of looking seriously into the mirror. If you are afraid to be open and receptive to what Spirit is trying to communicate, then you are not serious about awakening to your spiritual gift and honoring your mission in this life. Fear will have you placing your fingers in your ears to silence your higher self and block out the revelation.

Fear can cause you to hold on to the things that you know are not serving you well. You can feel within your heart that something is not for your highest good, but to release and let go would cause you to lose the very things that you have identified with for a very long time. The act of not-releasing stunts your growth. It's like being in a toxic relationship that is not equally yoked; you have feelings for each other, but you know that your spiritual path and your contribution to the world is not in alignment with how they see the world or their beliefs. To stay in this space would be detrimental to the soul and serve as the means to calcify connection with Source's energy and prevent the release of your healing gift. So you must *release* and *let go* of what's holding you back.

Marianne Williamson said, "Our deepest fear is not that we are inadequate. Our deepest fear is that we are powerful beyond measure. It is our light, not our darkness that most frightens us." The soul understands this to be true. Fear prevents you from Accepting the Call; we fear the unknown; we fear what we will become. No doubt, in truth, we fear what we already are. We fear the longing that calls out to us in the midnight hours, in the daily routines, in the quiet spaces. We fear the change that acceptance will bring about in our lives. To be truly accepting in the world is a radical shift for those accustomed to a legacy of judgment. To be truly ready for alignment, you have to be like the Fool and accept what is before you – and jump.

Fear is the opposite of compassionate love; compassion is a necessary grounding energy for healers. It requires a level of vulnerability and sensitivity. The challenge the reader may have is this idea of having compassion for people they feel are undeserving. No one is beneath or above the dignity of compassionate love. This grounding is healing for the healer as well as the querent. It's the key to connection and an essential element to your healing balm. Grounding in the Energy of Compassion will illuminate the fear and dispel the illusion of it by extending love.

Fear will keep us bound and feeling trapped like the Eight of Swords. To release your healing gift and expand to your healing path, you must embody the authority of your unique self- expression; you must honor your unique light. The fear of rejection can cause stagnation and prevent flowers from budding, deterring their fullest potential. If you don't embody the light that you are, your gifts do not pour from you effortlessly and easily; that means your waters are not flowing correctly, and fear is causing you to question your abilities. Once you embody the God-realized being you are – by expressing yourself without the negative chatter and need for approval – you have entered into a defining moment.

Fear will show up everywhere and nowhere; fear will have you full of anxiety about the unknown future; fear leads to thinking about what's next; fear will have no room for patience and precision focus. Having a focused will, void of fear, is an excellent building block for creation and manifestation. A focused will invites the universe to respond materially, so it is critical that we focus the will, deliberately. Focus the light by the power of the will.

In the end, fear prevents us from *trusting*. Fear will cancel out everything that has been requested of the universal consciousness. Fear is an indicator of doubt. It shows that you are not quite ready to just let go and trust that all will work out. We must have faith in the process, and with authority, focus the will, trusting in the manifesting power of your belief. The Tarot will help you uncover all your fears so that you can finally access the potential of your gifts and experience the longing finally fulfilled in your healing practice with yourself and others.

I've provided a Tarot spread called, "What must I release." The spread will help you get clear about the debilitating constructs that no longer serve you, and affords you a clear understanding of what it is you must release and let go to influence your transition into the healing arts.

Tarot Spread: Introduction of the Fool

The objective of the eight-card Releasing spread is to provide the querent the opportunity to gain clarity on *What is it that must be released and let go?* The Fool card serves as the dedicated significator card. This Major Arcana was chosen to represent freedom, fearlessness, adventure, and something new. It is the embodiment of carefree exploration. The Tarot spread asks the following:

1. 1. *What is it that I must let go, that I don't know I must let go?*
2. 2. *What is it that only I know I must let go?*
3. 3. *How do I feel about releasing and letting go?*
4. 4. *What will aid in my release?*
5. 5. *What happens if I let go?*
6. 6. *What happens if I do nothing and don't let go?*
7. 7. *What is the advice?*

Figure 7: The Releasing Spread

Preparing to Ground

Invocation of the Fool

As you begin your journey to connect and attune to the energy of the Fool, it's essential to create space to receive its insight. The initial step is the prayer of invocation. This is the point where you call upon the God of your understanding to intervene and come to your aid. The following prayer should be done before your meditation exercise and the drawing of cards. The ritual of prayer sets an intention and invites your team to assist you as you attempt to connect deeper to the Source that permeates all. Repeat the following prayer or replace it with one that resonates with you more.

> *Illuminate the road ahead. Make me ready for the journey. Clear the path of worry and lack, and remove all doubt and fears. – Ashe/Ase/Amen*

Meditation with the Fool

Remove the Fool card from the Tarot deck and place the card in your hand, on your lap, or under your pillow. Reposition your body in a sitting or lying position; it is paramount to align the spine in either case. Close your eyes, take three complete, full belly breaths, by inhaling through the nose and exhaling through the mouth. Return to normal breathing as you take your fourth breath and continue this circular breathing motion while relaxing your entire body. Let sweet relaxation wash over you, starting from the top of your head and proceeding down your shoulders, arms, hands, abdomen, thighs, and legs to the soles of your feet. Feel your body breathing. Feel that unseen force enter the physical body, expanding the diaphragm and feeling the sensation of this elemental force leaving the body temple. During this time, repeat aloud or in the mind's eye the mantra, "I am grounded in compassion." Thoughts may arise. Observe them, and let them pass away. You may hear sounds, see visions, smell a fragrance; allow all this to come and observe without judgment. You are now the witness, the observer. Continue to relax deeper and let go. Immediately following the meditation, take note of any impressions, messages, images, ideas, symbols, and inspirations that you received during this exercise and list any keywords, phrases, or thoughts. Ask yourself what words describe your feelings and/or any physical sensations you experienced during the meditation; you will use these details later to capture any themes and test for convergence.

Inquire of the Fool

Now that you have done the prayer of invocation, and have entered a state of meditation with the Fool, you are in the receptive mode. Take the Fool card, which will serve as the significator for this spread, and place it in the appropriate position as identified in the spread chart. Take the Tarot deck and shuffle, asking, "What is it that I must release and let go in this situation?" Once you have thoroughly shuffled the deck, cut the deck three times. Proceed to place the number of allotted cards according to the spread layout. I have provided an index to the Tarot cards' meanings in Chapter 4 to assist with interpretations. Once the cards are laid, list your initial impressions of the cards and any images that stand out, and then ascertain the actual meaning of the cards from the index.

Like the meditation exercise, create a list of words or phrases that describe your experiences with the cards.

Interpretation of Theme Convergence

Now that you have completed your list from your meditation and that you have completed your list based upon the Tarot spread, you will check for convergence or correspondence. You will be looking for things that are showing up in both your meditation and in the actual Tarot reading: those themes developed out of the lists of words or phrases, images, or symbols from both the meditation and the actual reading. The theme is the message or the communication; it is the answer to the question that you are seeking to illuminate. The goal here is to identify theme convergence and/or correspondence to corroborate the communication. Once this is done, use your intuition to determine the most reasonable and relevant messages you are receiving concerning your situation. This yields the interpretation.

The Releasing spread asks, *What is it that I must let go, that I don't know I must let go?* In an example reading, the card representing this inquiry is the Moon. The Moon indicates the querent's need to let go of fear and illusion. This card could be reflecting the fear of leaping into starting a part-time healing practice—the fear of not being good enough and the illusion of inadequacy. The second question asks, *What is it that only I know I must let go?* The card representing this inquiry is the Hermit. In this case, the Hermit indicates a period of isolation and withdrawal and the need to be alone. The message to the aspiring healer is, come down from the lonely mountain and share your healing light with the world. Let go of isolation. The third card asks, *how do I feel about releasing and letting go?* The card representing this inquiry is the Sun; it's a message to the healer of optimism and vitality. The querent is now feeling self-assured as a result of honoring true-self. The fourth card asks, *what will aid in my release?* The card representing this inquiry is Temperance. Temperance is saying to be confident. It's also about achieving balance and working with others by finding the middle ground. It will help if the querent remains open-minded. The fifth card asks, *what happens if I let go?* The card representing this inquiry is the Fool. The Fool represents adventure, and a new destination; there is no fear, only excitement about the new beginning. This new beginning is the aspiring healer's decision to learn Tarot reading. This is the aspiring healer developing marketing materials for their business, trying to turn leads into potential clients without fear of rejection. The final card asks, *what happens if I do nothing and don't let go?* The card representing this inquiry is the Ten of Swords; the message is you feel like a victim and are full of self-pity. This card indicates that if the querent does not act, they will feel powerless and bemoan their fate. There will be an increase in feelings of self-deprecation.

Practicing this spread will help you understand what energies you need to release and let go to become empowered as a healing practitioner. If you take note of the concepts that came up in the Tarot spread over time, you will see patterns emerge and be able to reconcile yourself with them. Studying this spread has allowed me to come to terms with people and attitudes that no longer serve me as I travel the healer's path of authority.

Affirmation of the Fool

Now that you have identified themes and have an interpretation, you are clear on the message, the insight, the lesson. The best way to actively practice and invoke this insight is to incorporate this into a daily affirmation practice. Based on the themes and the information you have received, you can now create your unique affirmation as a tribute to the Fool. This affirmation can be clear and simple: for example, "I am free, having no limitations or lack."

Now that we've covered the importance of releasing and letting go and started the work of identifying themes and solutions to releasing, let's put it all together.

Chapter 14

The Fool's Jump

*T*arot can provide transformative guidance to aspiring healing practitioners – those who feel called to the healing arts. Seven foundational insights can help you properly transition into your path of authority and the healing arts. These insights will allow you to prepare energetically for the lifelong task of embodying the divine healer. Internalizing and applying these insights is a path to clear confidence and security for the aspiring healer.

It is my wish that you begin to experience the preserving power that dwells within – knowing that that same preserving power will sustain all those who enter the healer's orbit. May you gain a strong sense of confidence and enthusiasm in expressing your gifts personally and professionally. Resting in your seat of authority gives you the confidence to know that you are secure, and that security manifests in the material and immaterial worlds. There is security in following the path of your highest calling.

The Tarot and the seven insights of Listening, Accepting, Grounding, Embodying, Focusing, Trusting, and Releasing can be transformative when incorporated into a budding healing practice. These insights support a healer's healing practice when starting a business in the healing arts. These insights provide the perfect conduit for developing your professional healing practice.

The Tarot is a healing modality that can support or complement any healing modality that you may employ in your professional practice. Learning from these insights will require a consistent Tarot practice, the goals being personal and professional development. This practice will be illuminating, and as you learn to connect with the cards, it will increase a great sense of confidence and establish a soul-felt connection to the Higher Power that is moving and shaping the world around you. If you follow these preparatory insights, you will begin the process of satisfying the deep longing within. I have no doubt you will unleash the lightworker – the divine healer within – and finally actively bring healing for yourself and your future clients.

I wrote this book as a testament to the great work that is ever-present in all the lives of God's creation. I wrote this book to serve as a reminder of the eternal hope that dwells in the gnawing to express your gift. However, that gift is manifested in this earthen form. Whatever that gift may be, the intended goals are to bring about the fullness of your being in this human experience, desiring to bring healing to the soul and through this, the transformation of humanity.

Thanks to the Source within for this truth that forever guides the souls, for a sail guided by the soul compass journeying to unknown lands.

I wrote this book for those who feel deep within that there is a purpose, a mission in this life that they must fulfill. They are not quite sure how to attain or achieve this aim, but they know deep within that there is something more profound than the existence they are currently undertaking. There's a feeling that continuously gnaws at you until you have achieved illumination, setting you right upon the path of perfect alignment.

Especially, I wrote this book to the man or woman who is languishing in a job, career, or profession that is no longer serving you. Perhaps it never served you in the first place. Perhaps it was merely a means to an end, and I would wager that end was survival, subsistence, and merely the pressure of expectation. However, outside all those external demands, you feel greatly that you have not lived up to your mission, your true calling, and you have not honored your healing gifts, in the many forms that they exist. The worldly possessions have created a wall, a barrier to the demonstration of your power.

I want you to know that it's never too late to invoke the eternal power. It's never too late to get in alignment with your higher calling. You can access your healing gift within, and you can practice your gift by healing yourself and others. I know that once you step your foot upon the plow, you can nourish the field of endless possibility and produce great things in this world, and among these works is a healing practice. You can start your healing business and help facilitate the healing of the world. You can achieve your full potential if you only become open and receptive to the possibility that it begins with a simple thought form manifested in the mind.

I wrote this book to share with the world a sacred tool that has helped to shape and guide me through the fogs of confusion, self-doubt, and fear. The Tarot provides sacred wisdom for healing, transformation, and illumination. This tool allows one to see the mirror of the soul. It allows you to be a witness to the true self, and it allows you the choice to respond to what you are seeing. I wrote this book to let people know that there is freedom in honoring the soul in the mirror; there is liberation is answering the healer's call.

Practice these insights through Tarot and become the healer you are called to be. Walk in your path of authority. The world is waiting for your healing light.

Appendix

Key to the Spreads

The Listening Spread

Chapter 7. Listen to Still, Small Voice (Get in the Receptive Mode)
What is it that I need to hear concerning this situation?

S. The High Priestess
1. What impedes my hearing – keeps me from being in the receptive mode?
2. What is the message from the Higher Consciousness that I have not been hearing?
3. What's the lesson/insight to be gained?

Chapter 8. Accepting the Call (Pick up the Phone)
What must I accept?

 Or  Or

S. The Tower / Death / The Hanged Man
1. What is that I know I must accept?
2. What are the consequences of not accepting?
3. How will I feel when I accept?
4. What's the Advice?

Chapter 9. Grounding in the Energy of Compassion (Love Is the Way)

Towards what do I need to show compassion?

S. Strength
1. Towards what do I need to be compassionate?
2. What challenges my grounding?
3. What grounds me?
4. What's the insight/advice?

Chapter 10. Embody the Authority of Self- Expression (I Am the Light)

How can I embody my authority?

S. Emperor
1. What is my authority?
2. What challenges my authority?
3. What enhances my authority?
4. What will align me with my authority?
5. What is the insight/lesson?
6. Outcome

Chapter 11. Focusing the Will (Will Power)
What's my focus?

S. The Chariot
1. **What is my focus at present?**
2. **Where should I focus going forward?**
3. **What would compromise my focus?**
4. **What is the insight/lesson?**

Chapter 12. Trust (Have Faith)
What should I trust?

S. The Star
1. What do I trust that at present is not serving me?
2. Where should I place my trust?
3. What compromises/challenges my trust?
4. What is the insight?
5. What's the outcome?

Chapter 13. Release and Let Go
What is it that I must release and let go?

 Or

S. The Fool / The Hanged Man
1. What is it that I must let go, that I don't know I must let go?
2. What is it that I only know I must let go?
3. How do I feel about releasing and letting go?
4. What will aid in my release?
5. What happens if I let go?
6. What happens if I do nothing and don't let go?
7. What is the advice

Acknowledgment

Thanks to my Godparents Rosalyn and Francis Priester. I have no words to express my love and sincere appreciation for taking me in as your son. I'm so fortunate to be able to call you mother and father. Pops, thanks for teaching me to take the lesson as the blessing.

To Debra Nichols Windham, my Godmother and sixth-grade teacher, who never gave up on me even when I kept making the same mistake on my essays. Thank you for giving me my very first thesaurus. I turned out to be real "eccentric."

To Peter Woods (Pedro), my God dad, thanks for taking me in as your own and loving me equally as your own flesh and blood. I hope I've made you proud.

Special thanks to my Godbrother Jeremy Woods, and Godsister Starlet Windham for allowing me to call you brother and sister. I love you both immensely.

To Ms. Elois Goon, my Social Science professor at Kennedy King College: I will never forget the meal you provided and the call you made to me to ensure I honored my civic duty and registered to vote. Thanks for showing real love and genuine concern for your students.

To Dr. AJ Stovall, Ms. Stovall, and Dr. James Mock, my political and social science professors from Rust College, who allowed me the opportunity to study abroad in West Africa. Life-changing. Thank you for teaching me the importance of scholarship and loving myself as an African man.

To the Rev. Dr. Jeremiah A. Wright, Jr., thank you for teaching me about the unconditional love of God and allowing me to know that "different does not mean deficient."

To Valeria Davis, who gave me my very first part-time job my freshmen year, working for the Illinois State Rep. Charles G. Morrow III office as the Legislative Student Aid. That opportunity would guide the direction of my academic and professional career.

To Greg King of State Farm Insurance, thank you for your mentorship and for being an example of a successful businessman.

To Aunt Brenda Vance, I sincerely love you. Thank you for praying for me and teaching me how to inhale Jesus and exhale the ego-self. You are one of my biggest role models. The lessons that you tried to teach me still rest upon my heart.

To Frank Clark, a fellow alumnus of Hirsch High school, thanks for giving me your card in the school library those so many years ago. You gave me my first real job in corporate America and allowed me the privilege of developing life-long mentors like George Lofton and Todd Banks.

Todd Banks, the mentor of mentors, what can I say, I love you! You have been by my side for so many years. Thank you for firing me so many years ago. It was the best thing you could have done. The tough love was life-changing.

To Mark Sims, my very first mentor, I met you in elementary school through the Black Star Mentor Program. You taught me that if I ever needed anything, I should "learn how to write." I took it literally, and as a kid, when I needed anything of importance like a summer job, help with getting in college, or a sponsor for my Beta Club trips, I would write letters to people like Al Gore, Arnie Duncan, Oprah. Thanks for sowing the seed of writing.

To Janene Jackson, I love you more than words can express. Thank you for believing in me and taking a chance on me. You will never know how much you saved my life and changed it for the better, my angel.

To my biological brother Ashley D. Weaver, you are a walking talent. I love you. Thank you for teaching me the lesson of Temperance. If not for your lesson, I would not be the refined conduit for healing I am today.

To my Khosi Mpho Malie, my king of kings: thanks for allowing me the experience of a healthy love and for teaching me how to have a constructive conversation. You are forever in my heart and always my friend.

To my team of guides, ancestors, angels, nature spirits: I'm eternally grateful for your continued presence, love, and unwavering, always at-the-ready, support and guidance.

To my friend Ricky D. Talley, I love you, I love you, I love you. You have been one of my biggest supporters and a loyal friend. Thank you for believing in me and traveling the highways and byways with me to every expo and every festival. You have been by my side since day one of this healing journey. You are my angel, and I honor you, mighty lion.

To Reginald Davis my March 1st Pisces twin, my oldest hometown (Chicago) friendship. Thanks for being such a supportive and honorable friend; our relationship is invaluable to me.

To Mareco A. Knox, thanks for being one of my oldest and best friends. Our relationship means the world to me. You inspire me to be the best that I can be in this human experience.

You are a beast, you are the strong Bull, and when it comes to business, I love the hustle, and I love you.

To Beverly Hitchins, thank you for reminding me of my light and being such an open and receptive mentor and teacher. You are the wise Queen of Swords, and I honor you.

To Howard Lee (Howie), thank you for your expert advice, technical support, and service referrals. You are one of the major reasons why I have an online platform.

To my editor, Anna Paradox, what can I say? You are awesome! I appreciate the depth of our connection, thanks for believing in my message and perfecting my voice. Divine Order brought us together right one time.

There are so many more, and you know who you are. Please know that you are loved and appreciated.

About the Author

$\mathcal{Z}$achary Weaver, Ph.D., known as Dr. Z, hails from Chicago, IL, and is currently residing in Washington, DC, serving as a Tarotist and Reiki Practitioner. *Tarot & the Healing Arts* is his first book.

Dr. Z gained the name the "Tarot Teddy Bear" due to his gentle nature. He exudes an effortless humility matched with tenderness and a deep emotional sensitivity for others. His energy provides a sense of comfort and security. Dr. Z's gentleness reminds all who experience him of the freedom and security that come from being vulnerable. His essence offers a profound calm, which allows for an open heart when perceiving a situation. He's a being of compassion, authority, and authentic self-expression.

Known as a healer, he works with clients from all walks of life, to bring clarity and direction when navigating the ever-changing winds of life. He's passionate about helping people change their lives for their highest good. Serving and supporting people (as they journey through the terrain of human experiences) is his life purpose.

Dr. Z is a self-taught healing practitioner. For the past twenty years, he has studied esoteric teachings both formally and informally. He is a certified Oneness Deeksha Giver and Reiki practitioner, a member of the American Tarot Association, and of the Tarosophy Tarot Association. He holds a Bachelor of Arts in Political Science from Rust College, a Master of Public

Administration from Clark Atlanta University, and Doctorate in Public Policy Administration from Walden University.

Dr. Z uses the Tarot as a tool to tap into divine wisdom. He views Tarot reading as an access point, an evidence of a stream of energetic interconnectedness, serving as a conduit for accessing universal consciousness, where infinite knowledge exists. Tarot is a tool for illumination and transformation. Tarot's very demonstration affirms all life's connection to an invisible web of spiritual wisdom. This knowledge can be targeted and downloaded. Dr. Z. reveals the path before you by showing you the light within. The Tarot Teddy Bear illuminates the way, by sharing divine guidance on every question about work, home, fortune, love, and more. His experience proves that Tarot can illuminate your present condition, by observing the current direction of the arcana and that Tarot can light the transformational paths available to you, as you journey through this moment that is the human experience. Let the Tarot Teddy Bear be your guide!

Thank You

$\mathcal{Y}$ou made it through the book – congratulations! As a thank you for your commitment, I would like to offer you a free bonus Tarot spread. To get your copy go to my website at the link below.

Dr. Z Tarot Consulting

P.O. Box 62498

Washington, DC 20019

Office: 202-599- 0285

ZDW@DrZTarot.com

WWW.DrZTarot.com